Lost Reality

Thomas Medonis

Good Word Books

2015

What Runs Through Our Minds

Totalitarian:[1]

1.

of or pertaining to a centralized government that does not tolerate parties of differing opinion and that exercises dictatorial control over many aspects of life.

2.

exercising control over the freedom, will, or thought of others; authoritarian; autocratic.

---

[1] http://dictionary.reference.com Howard Zinn also began *A Power Governments Cannot Suppress* in this manner

Table of Contents:

Death in Adolescence

A sudden dip prevailed as the wind led the disc to a five foot descent. This change of flight forced the heavy sprint to become one of full extension. The Frisbee still remained twenty feet away. The arm pumps could not extend any further. Accompanied with breaths becoming sporadically heavier, Thomas Adams was now running as fast as he could. Uncertainty had begun to set in. Failure was not an option. He could not let the Frisbee hit the ground. A momentous leap seemed to be all that would make or break his chances with the one that he coveted yet never spoke to.

Expertise had been acquired through many nights of tossing the biz on the campus of Springfield College. Outside of the dorms Tom's time was spent with his particular group of roommates and friends, otherwise known as Jerrytown. This group, which congregated on the green in front of Tom's dorm, consisted mostly of hippies, with some coordinated mystics and jocks mixed in. They played entirely on campus with the exception of Forest Park. Jerrytown, the intramural ultimate Frisbee championship team, first formed sophomore year. Years of practice consequently led Tom to believe he would somehow reach Fitzy's long throw in the beginning of their final fall semester.

The common man would have given up thirty feet prior. Long strides had gotten him this far. Now there was no time for another step. His right arm straightened and stretched out an extra foot the moment his horizontal body paralleled the ground. A perfect line formed all the way from his erect middle finger down to his pointed toes- an arrow at full torque.

The lone focal spectator would watch the near impossible feat vividly. With the meeting point approaching, she raptly fixated on the point of improbability.

Hips make first contact, directly followed by elbow and knees.

Whitney stood over. "Wow!" she said.

The disc was now one foot off the ground, held upright in the perpendicular right arm of Thomas Adams.

It was achieved- success!

The Frisbee was prevented from a landing upon the pristine college grass.

"What a catch!" Whitney, the short-haired, skinny, highlighted blonde said. The attractive twenty-year-old towered over Tom's backside- with hands on her hips. His over sized cargo shorts had slipped down his thighs. Red and blue checkered boxers were in Whitney Stanton's sight.

Tom, at once, turned over onto his rear still holding the Frisbee and sat up. The grass stains became evident on slender knees and cargoes that pointed toward the sky. No words accompanied the first glance at Whitney, just a wide smile.

"I didn't think I was going to reach that one," Tom finally spit out.

"Yeah Tommy!" Fitzy's words were muffled from afar. Christopher Fitzgerald was the only member of Jerrytown present in front of the townhouses throwing the biz with Tom. Naturally for the two, they were throwing the biz in front of the Townhouses on this Tuesday afternoon. Fitzy was one-half of Tom's two roommates, Mike Williams was the other. Mike though was back in Town House Three researching who supplied Springfield College's drinking water.

Fitz, by far, was one of the most vocal in Jerrytown. The large set young man, whose stretched fingers held the same width as the Frisbee, was by far the only conservative within the group. He had a "right-wing" opinion on every topic.

Christopher Fitzgerald was too a social butterfly, and Tom wasn't. The moment Fitz saw the girl Tom fancied he came up with the clever smokescreen in order to commence an advance. Tom's sprint had ulterior motives, rather than just catching a Frisbee.

An instant link ensued subsequent to the catch, but Tom still was a little embarrassed with his effort. And it was all because of Fitzy's improvisation to send Tom on this impossible feat. Something Tom would never have thought of to simply create an interaction.

On the ground with Whitney looking down, Tom thought to himself, "Normal people don't randomly dive at Frisbees on a Tuesday afternoon."

This young man at first glimpse seemed like any other fit twenty-one year old college student- tight fade, Birkenstock clogs, cargo shorts, and a bulky hemp necklace that encircled the collar of a Bird jersey. A patchy brown scruff filled his cheeks and chin albeit was not foregoing a beard.

Deep down past the attractiveness, was a sad sad uncertain boy however. Wounds from year's prior still were sore. Tom had not healed yet. He did not know the proper way to fix the damage his father had done. Oh how his environment had shaped him. Was the American dream still available for this young man?

Beyond the scars and pain, a superficial indescribable energy Thomas discharged, which Whitney noticed long before this diving catch during the beginning of their senior year. It was clear he was far different from the others.

Prior to the dive, Tom had never been in love. No commitments were ever made to another, never feeling an inkling of romantic chemistry. Experiences thus far in regards to love had been anything but the one emotion that can change the world. A muddled interpretation evolved on the matter of commitment and matrimony. Marriage for his parents was a clear indication of the society he had lived in. It had failed.

His parents divorced when he was eleven during extreme dysfunction. An event the senior had yet coped with or settled. Let alone parents separating, his father was the town drunk everyone knew of in Hartford, and Hartford is a very large city. His mother Wendy tried and tried and tried to salvage something out of nothing. The time came though when hope was gone.

Obviously, embarrassment, jealousy, and resentment could not be avoided during Tom's youth.

Robert Adams, Tom's father, died of alcoholism at the age of forty-one in November 1996. Robert's death occurred Tom's freshman year when was attending Bulkeley High School in Hartford, Connecticut.

It was very difficult for Wendy not to feel relief. By no means was her ex-husband a means for support-emotionally or financially. Wendy Adams', on the contrary, supported Tom as a single-mother police officer.

Before his death, the living arrangements set up a very awkward scenario for Robert, Wendy, and Tom after the divorce in 1995, while the family lived in the south end of Hartford. Parents were no longer together, yet they still lived under the same roof. Robert would call the seasonally sweltering, or frigid, attic home.

Robert lived a sad life. The only time he was seen out of the house during his final years was during his walks to find booze or get his minimal turkey dinner at the diner. That was the extent of his existence. Wendy worked the midnight shift, which allowed the strange living conditions to work. She simply avoided Robert by sleeping during the day. Her motivation rested on saving enough money to leave her ex-husband's house and buy a house in a better school district for Tom.

Yes, the two tried their hardest to avoid each other, but Tom would not avoid the drunk. Daily visits upstairs would be made under the illusion that Tom wanted to listen to a rare record of his Dad's massive collection. Being intoxicated, Robert didn't mind the visit and actually the encounter was the lone enjoyment he held in his rotten state. His condition consistently declined, with his habit increasing each day. Robert was very fortunate that he was not homeless.

Robert and Wendy inherited the two-family house from Robert's father, Gus, when Tom was an infant in 1982. Gus Adams had previously bought the house in Hartford under the assumption that it would be a profitable investment, but renting it out and maintaining it had become too great a responsibility for the elder. Ever since Gus first bought the house, the first floor was rented out to an elderly woman, Miss Harriet Foley, who had lived on the first floor through the several changes in owners since 1970.

She was a retired school principal, single and never married. More or less, she lived the life of a nun. There were daily church visits. Through the years of his growth, Foley took a liking to Tom, always inviting him in the moment he walked up the front steps. She would always follow the greeting by reiterating the necessity to read. "Thomas," the hunched back old lady would call him, "reading will open all your doors."

The strong relationship between boy and Foley, ironically, first began as a result of Tom's destruction. An eight year-olds apology due to cracking his downstairs neighbor's window would be the first lengthy encounter the two would hold. Subsequently, Miss Foley's first floor back window would be shattered ten more times through the years. Yes, friendship arose all because of a rubber baseball that was supposed to be rebounding against the wood siding. Still, it was never a problem. She was only concerned that Thomas told her soon after the damage happened.

Ms. Foley was well aware there was a problem with Tom's father ever since the family moved in. She had seen many addict parents come and go through the school system. The frail jaundice bald alcoholic was always loud and angry, but she didn't pry. Nearly each time Tom was down by the circumstances of the times, he seemed to bump into Ms. Foley in front of the house. The elder would ask if he wanted to talk over some Oreo's. Looking into her thick glasses, he would always respond in the same manner, "I don't want to bother you. I'm just having a bad day."

"I have some nice horticulture magazines to show you!" she would respond.

It worked every time. Tom would spend hours looking at magazines while dipping his cookies in milk on the first floor. Never a mention of his father though.

Robert was very sly in that he would visit Miss Foley's door the first of every month in order to receive the rent money. During the marriage, he would leave two hundred in an envelope for Wendy, for utilities and living expenses, and then pocket the rest of the rent money. The remainder was then used for his booze until it ran dry by the end of the month. The cycle would again repeat.

He would never give his wife any additional money while the two were married. The moment Wendy told Robert she wanted a divorce, though, he came up with an agreement that would compensate her with some extra money and free housing, all the while lawyers remained out of it. Truly, Robert did not want to lose the home. Deep down Robert acknowledged that he could not maintain it without Wendy's assistance.

Robert made it very clear during every nasty argument subsequent to the divorce that he was doing Wendy a favor by letting her board for free in "my house." It was the most dysfunctional situation, but Tom's mom Wendy, who hated the man, had nowhere else to go. Everything he promised when they were young never came true- aside from their beautiful boy.

Tom, naturally, adored his father for the longest time. As a child his father was superman- he could do no wrong. Through time, however, Tom would grow ashamed of what truly existed. The process of an ugly divorce behind closed doors was a clear indication of what truly existed. All of his classmates, who had living arrangements not nearly as strange as his, made Tom quite aware of his situation.

One day at the age of twelve, with innocence fading, Tom gained the courage to faintly call out his father. He sporadically wrote a bold note in capital letters. The powerful sign was pinned at eye level on the outside of his father's attic door:

DAD, I WILL NOT TALK TO YOU IF YOUR DRUNK AGAIN TOMORROW,

FROM YOUR SON.

Tom could not withstand the arguments or shame any longer. Robert, nonetheless, had no ability to sense what was being placed on his door at eight in the evening while he lay incapacitated. As Tom pushed the thumbnail, undistinguishable Blues was blasting from behind the door. The twelve year old no longer could keep the anguish in and immediately broke down. All the pain and sadness came out. He couldn't make it any further than the bottom steps of the stairwell leading out to the second floor. He sat and wept into his forearms for ten minutes while shrugging over his knees. He sat sobbing so loud neighbors could hear him, but in his home no one could hear, mom was sleeping, dad wasn't conscious. This was the only time his father made him cry.

His father obviously read the note. It was removed the following day, but all to no avail. Yes, it made Robert sad, but his only solution for sorrow was booze.

Tom, consequently, no longer grieved at age twelve. He had given up on his father's state improving.

Nevertheless, life for Tom continued with dysfunction and worry everyday. More anxiety though was spent upon his mother's profession rather than Robert's condition. Wendy had sacrificed her safety for the public's- all in order to give Tom a normal childhood. A female police officer working the midnight shift would draw fear in any offspring. Tom was no exception. He spent every evening creating negative scenarios while his mother was away at work- consistently staying awake until 3 in the morning.

She was stuck though. Robert did not fulfill his share of the marriage and put all the stress on a young mother, who was willing to work through any problem as long as Robert was sober. Still, while she lived rent free she saved and saved and saved. Yes, she could have rented, but she thought that as a waste of money. She wanted to be a homeowner. Deep down, also, she didn't want Robert to be alone.

In Robert's reality, through his charitable contribution of Ms. Foley's rent check to his family, he thought of himself as a saint. With such varying opinions, the arguments were very potent during the early stages of the divorce, in which Robert made very clear he did not owe Wendy a dime for 'the kid'. It was more than enough to give them a roof over their head for free.

High School

All through this adolescent difficulty, an incessant thought would replay in Tom's mind, "I will never be like him."

Avoidance from alcohol throughout high school would come easy. His mother administered a judicial omnipresence upon her only child. Filling the male void along with working in law enforcement shaped an exceptionally sturdy woman. Becoming a cop was the only means in which the medium build high school educated single mother found she could support a growing boy and buy a house. All the same, the midnight shift did take a toll on their relations.

With great development in motion, an additional worry would be stirred inside Tom. His mother began dating a man with Robert still alive. She was over Robert. There was no more love she could provide him with. William Curtis would quickly fill the empty void. He was a detective from the neighboring precinct. Every date night Wendy was treated like gold; even though she didn't cry out for any nurturing. Tom needed a father figure and for Wendy, Detective Curtis fit the bill. Fortunately, nothing was ever exposed to Robert. On off nights, Wendy attended the dates. As things seemed positive subsequent to a couple dates, Tom joined his mother and the detective for dinner. It was a bit uncomfortable for the teen, especially for the fact that Tom promised to never tell his father.

The opposite of Wendy's intentions occurred however. The knowledge of his mother dating brought great pain in Tom. Even if Wendy dated Jesus, her only son would still have been heartbroken. It was not his father. At thirteen, Tom asked his mother before she left for work one night, "Mom, please promise to never date again."

"I can't do that. It's hard to be alone," she responded.

All this weight compiled inside carried over into adulthood. Emotions would be weaved and tangled together. Yet, he unconditionally loved his mother like no other. A big kiss would be presented on his mother's cheek every night, as Tom was still awake when Wendy would leave for work at eleven p.m. Wendy didn't know that Tom would stay up every night agonizing over a hypothetical phone call related to her safety.

Usually Wendy's mother, Ann, would stay over. However, there were instances Tom was alone all night, as Robert was in no position for security.

Obviously, the drunk did not get along with his ex-mother-in-law. Seclusion was sought whenever she was over. If there were ever a circumstance when the two interacted- a toilet clogged or air conditioning trouble-an argument would ensue. Grandma Ann would always take a couple days off if Robert gave her grief. "Wendy, I'm not dealing with that man ever again." But she returned. Ann Jackson, who divorced as well, lived in a small one bedroom condo, in which there was no possibility Wendy could move in with Thomas.

It was a very ill at ease situation on everyone, but since the house was in Robert Adams' name he felt empowered. But Robert died in 1996 and things quickly changed.

Wendy made a rare visit to the attic to discuss the whereabouts of the most recent rent money, but instead of resolving the matter, she discovered her limp ex. There was blood everywhere. Wendy, practicing her profession, quickly learned the source for the mess upon the sheets. Life for Robert ended with a four inch wrist slit.

The moment Robert succumbed to life was near midnight while Tom was still awake. White linen would increase in saturation, while he finally slept and then left for school. Discovery wasn't until Wendy awoke from her three hour rest after the midnight shift. Fortunately, Tom was at school during the scream of his mother.

It was November freshman year at Bulkeley High School when he was called to the office. Previous to this point, Tom was picked on and immensely embarrassed about his life. Another incident made known at school wouldn't help his ego.

In little league his father sat at the same bench every time overlooking the field. He would be so obnoxious that teammates would form great anecdotes toward poor Tom- D.D. for "drunken daddy" or "coach alchy". The youth couldn't even have friends over. The house was always a mess. Wendy had no time to clean the mess Tom and his father would make. Nor had Tom the opportunity to develop a cleaning discipline. Hence, the only time the house was cleaned was by his grandmother. There was one instance a friend stopped by when no one was home and the front door was unlocked. The house was a disaster. The following day at school Tom learned from every classmate just how dirty his house was.

The call his mother made into school on November 21st would only increase his insecurity. The instant Mrs. Mathews, Tom's history teacher, hung up the phone with the secretary; she told Tom he was wanted in the office. Somehow he knew. Intuition expressed his father was gone during the longest fifty foot walk he had ever taken.

"Tom, come in here, take a seat after you close the door," the principal shouted out to Tom as he entered the waiting room.

"How's freshman year?" The overweight white principal had asked.

"Oh good, Mr. Deustch. Is everything OK? Why am I here?" Tom asked.

"Well, we are just waiting for your mother."

Within a few minutes of small talk Wendy walked in holding a morbid gesture.

"Mom what's wrong?"

"Its your father, he's dead."

Tom rose, "How?"

"Alcohol. The Liver," she said.

"Oh." The youth sat down without a tear in his eye.

Principal Deustch quickly intervened. He discussed coping with the matter for a few minutes, in which every recommendation was followed with a head bob from Tom. Tom just wanted to get home and shut his bedroom door to keep away.

The wake and funeral went very fast. Tom did not tell anyone about the services. Not many people came out, which was what Tom wanted. At this stage, Wendy knew something had to change. Thus, it was decided this would be Tom's final year in the city. Wendy was going to use her modest savings in turn to move to a better school district. She was going to ask her mother to move into the two family house for the time being,

and then join her daughter and grandson move into a
new home.

This final year in Hartford was very difficult for
Tom. It was freshman year in a high school where he
was one of fifteen white kids in a school that exceeded
twelve hundred in enrollment. On only one day his
freshman year he wasn't called a 'cracker'.

Hartford High stimulated much more
embarrassment and insecurities the remainder of his
first year. Insults on his color or, even worse, what
happened to his father, ran constant. Students knew
what had happened, all Tom's peers from elementary
and middle school were most aware. On the outside,
Tom didn't seem phased; he simply ignored the ill
human nature. But inside he was overwhelmed with
discomfort.

A few students, however, made Tom feel alright.
Paul, for instance, would have Tom over his house a
couple times a week after school to play basketball. Tom

would even try out for the high school freshman team only to quit after the first week of tryouts.

One Hispanic student, Jose, also helped Tom make it through. Tom would walk home a mile some days with Jose, who lived down the road from him. As they walked, passing by dreadful abandoned dwellings, Tom became very paranoid by the other cultures huddled outside. Tom would whisper to Jose, "They're going to kill me!"

But Jose would reassure him, "You're with me, you're fine."

The school year was quite difficult but he made it through. Early summer the move came into fruition. With the end of freshman year came a fresh start. In the last week of school, Tom was told that they were moving out of Hartford. Now that the house was in Tom's name, along with Wendy's savings, a move was possible. Wendy put a hefty down payment on the new purchase in Wethersfield, while taking on a fifteen year mortgage.

Ultimately, she found a house half a mile south of Hartford in suburban Wethersfield. And so, the summer was full of moving, painting, and decorating. Such a short distance travelled for such a drastic change. Tom loved his new house and three-quarters an acre. There were, however, some adjustments to be made subsequent from departing the city. Sophomore year in a new school was far different from anything he ever knew. Yes, he was only a half-mile from his old school, but he was now part of the majority. The demographics were flip flopped. There were now only twenty-three minorities attending Wethersfield High School.

At first, in the first September weeks of school Tom befriended kids who were not on the right side of the tracks. For some reason Tom was attracted to the troubled kids. With two other white students, Sam and Scott, Tom would spend his time after school. There was much more freedom in Wethersfield. The three would walk behind the school into the wooded trail called "Folly Brook" nearly everyday. Either Sam or Scott would have a pack of Newport's. Each and every time Tom would graciously refuse though.

Wendy could sense Tom was becoming guilty by association whenever the three would come to Tom's house on Church Street. However, there was little she could do. She was sleeping most of the time Tom was meandering in the new home, eliminating any opportunity to monitor her only child's behavior or peers.

There was one saving grace, which began as a petty bet in November. Tom found wrestling. The sport was quite foreign to the sophomore. He was clearly unfamiliar with it in gym class. He had no idea what a double leg take down or a sprawl was. Yet, within a week of practicing the plethora of moves taught in class, he began to enjoy rolling around with classmates. As Tom completed a perfect fireman's carry in class the last day of covering wrestling, Mr. Flannigan, the gym teacher, stopped Tom pinning his opponent and said, "Wow, I'll make a bet with you Tom. I bet you can't make it through a whole season. One-hundred dollars, it starts next week."

Getting involved in a positive extracurricular activity was all the result of a potential Mr. Flannigan had saw in the teen. The gym teacher was also the wrestling coach. Wrestling thus started out as a good distraction to keep him away from trouble and substance during a critical year of growth. In the first week of practice, which started the week after Thanksgiving, Tom was a bit overprotective. He didn't let any fellow teammates in or say much. In addition, the crap was beat out of him during the first week on the mat.

Soon thereafter, once Coach Flannigan had the wrestlers' wrestle live against their similar sized partner, Tom began to feel comfort and opened up. A strong fondness for his teammates ensued, which led him to spend most of his time alongside them throughout the year, not only during wrestling season. His team was not that good, but for some reason Tom gradually became a wonderful talent. However, not starting the sport until sophomore year, which is a rather late time to learn a highly technical sport, made the first season quite trying.

Coach Jim Flannigan was a larger than average white male. The man, who originated from Harrisburg, Pennsylvania, was about six foot, two hundred pounds. Flannigan had been recruited to wrestle at Central Connecticut State University. He then decided to stay in the nutmeg state. Flannigan was a very proactive coach, wherein he would roll around with the athletes nearly every practice. Experiencing the skill of Flannigan was very beneficial for his wrestlers.

Coach knew what Tom had experienced the prior year with the death of his father and wanted to help. Tom, however, would not talk about any of it. He kept everything in at first. Slowly however, with Monday through Saturday practices, matches, and tournaments, Tom became very comfortable around the thirty year old coach.

Flannigan knew he found something very special. Tom was very athletic, but prior to wrestling, he was doing nothing with it. He would try sports in prior years, but he would never stick with anything. He did not play any one sport for more than a season. It was obvious to Flannigan that Tom was down in the dumps when he arrived in Wethersfield and would head on the devious path if he hung out with the wrong crowd. As gossip prevailed, there wasn't a student throughout the school who didn't know Tom's story. He was now too ashamed of who he was in a new district.

Tom was a good looking kid- sturdy. The outside saw he held great potential, but the most important person did not see it. In recognition of this, Flannigan made the hundred dollar bet with some oblique motives.

Great uncertainty accompanied the nerves, but Tom took on the bet and didn't miss one practice or match. The sophomore wrestling season, however, was a disappointment in terms of results. Tom only won two matches out of thirty. More importantly, Tom befriended some teammates. With the prolonged bus rides and Saturday tournaments bonding was unavoidable.

And so, Flannigan was a man of his word. Tom was handed a hundred dollar bill the moment he was eliminated from the state tournament. Yet, Tom wanted more. Not money, but wrestling. The sport stuck with Tom even with the modest win percentage. Improvement became a focal point in order to stand atop the podium as the state champs had.

He would attend open mats at Wethersfield High, overseen by Flannigan and neighboring coaches, during the entire summer. He also put strenuous work in on his conditioning (running and lifting). One hundred pull ups a day were put into the routine as well. By junior year his confidence, conditioning, and style all underwent a metamorphose. As a seventh seed he wrestled his way into the state finals. He lost, but he still took second in the states. It was a wonderful second year of wrestling.

Tom continued to wrestle, run, and lift in the off-season before his final high school season. By senior year he became a state champ. He had a straightforward style. Opponents could not contend with his explosive takedowns. The moment the one hundred forty pounder walked off the mat with a pin in the state finals, he jumped upon Flannigan and gave him a huge embrace around his neck.

In terms of the nation, Connecticut was a weak wrestling state, nothing like Ohio, New Jersey, Pennsylvania, etc. Nevertheless, Tom propelled himself to the top of Connecticut in what he thought was his final season of wrestling. Tom peaked at the end of the season; when it all mattered.

One of the few college coaches that recruited from the Connecticut State Tournament in hopes of recruiting a state champ saw Tom wrestle. The collegiate coach knew instantly that Tom was a special talent. At the time Tom hadn't any plan for after high school, probably the military. When he was asked by Coach Bly, during a break in the tourney, if he was interested in wrestling for Springfield College, he responded, "I sure am." Through this opportunity Tom would become the first member of his family to attend college. All of his cousin's were either in the military or abusing substance.

The summer before freshman year of college was lackluster. Tom avoided all the big parties while remaining in very good shape, conditioning every day. He didn't make any really close friends in his three years at Wethersfield. A couple girls came and went, but none stuck. College was a new beginning, a new frontier. The eighteen year old stood on the same stage as the other freshman.

He made the choice to study landscape architecture and plant science. They were strange majors for a city boy with no agricultural experience, but he loved nature, especially trees. He was also working as a groundskeeper during the summer.

Every week the teen's favorite places to travel on bike from Wethersfield into Hartford were Bushnell Park and Cedar Hill Cemetery; both landscapes designed by Jacob Weidenmann, an immigrant from Switzerland in 1856. Tom learned from Ms. Foley that Bushnell park was designed in 1860 and Cedar Hill Cemetery in 1863. Cedar Hill was the final resting place for his father.

Freshman Year

With this great respect and passion for natural aesthetics, he too wanted to influence the art within nature. And so, Tom sent in his letter and grades to Springfield College- the top plant science school in New England. Coach Bly assured him via phone that he would get in no problem with his C average along with the Nine-fifty on his SAT's. Truth be told, Tom would not have even considered college had he not been recruited. He would have chosen the military. It seemed to be the correct path for a lot of other kids.

Moving in time came the last week in August. He was chosen to live in International Hall, a towering dorm with eight floors. Tom had his roommate randomly selected, which Coach Bly had some influence in. Nicholas Pace was the young man chosen to share a fifteen by twelve block room.

Fortunately, Tom and Nick lived on the second floor, making moving in much easier than if they lived on the seventh floor. Tom and his mother first carried up the suitcases of clothes after he checked in with the Resident Director to get his key. The RD said that his roommate already checked in, which brought excitement to Tom. 212 was a middle room.

With the turn of a key, Nick appeared on his bed with the TV on. The two quickly introduced themselves. They initially shot the breeze about their own wrestling accomplishments. Coach Bly had prior informed the two that they would be sharing a room with a possible teammate.

Nick's persona did not appear favorable for Wendy however. His shaggy hair and demeanor appeared to be that of a burnout, which she was very familiar with in her line of work. After the look over, Wendy interrupted the two to tell Tom, she was going to get more things from her car. Nick never offered to help. As the two were loading things in the room through several trips, Nick whispered to Tom with Wendy out at the car, "You smoke?"

"Never," Tom said.

"Look at this." Nick showed Tom his bubbler.

"What does that do?"

"Get's you high man!" Nick said, "You have a lot to learn greeny."

And so, with a kiss on his forehead, Wendy was gone. Tom was now living on his own. Yes, Tom had experienced many things others with two stable parents had not. In some areas he had developed superior traits, while in others he held inferior traits. One for instance, was expressing himself. He kept everything in. He felt shame his entire adolescence. It was going to take a long time to change his mindset. Most important for Tom in becoming comfortable in his own skin was meeting positive people- comfort not anxiety.

Tom would find Fitzy and Mike freshman year, wherein a friendship for the duration of college began.

Mike was the same build as Tom, but he had dark curly hair that never grew longer than his ears or eyebrows. He was from New Jersey where wrestling took priority over every other sport. Mike was one of Coach Bly's top recruits for Springfield College. Even in the weight class below Tom, Mike was still a much better wrestler. Entering college Mike was very confident he was going to be an All-American. Springfield was a division three school, while most of his teammates from high school went to the more competitive DI or DII colleges. Wrestling would turnout, however, much different than what he first expected.

Tom met Fitzy and Mike at the first wrestling team meeting for freshman only, wherein Nick also attended. Mike, Fitz, and Tom all lived in different dorms freshman year. The freshman group would meet a couple weeks subsequent to their arrival at Springfield College. Great uncertainty of what to expect from the winter sport was held by every freshman sitting on the wrestling mat in the complete red padded wrestling room. Mike Williams and the heavyweight Christopher Fitzgerald sat on opposite sides of Tom while Nick distanced himself.

Fitzy would continuously present anecdotes to Mike and Tom about the dwarf-sized coach. While Coach John Bly overdramatically expressed his expectations toward the incoming freshman with constant hand gestures, Fitzy was comparing the bald headed, full grey beard, Bly, to a flying squirrel. Fitzy also made it clear during a brief break in the meeting that he wasn't going to wrestle. "This meeting is a waste of my time, I gotta get a drink after this. You boys wanna join? Gotta thirty rack in the room!"

"Sure," nodded Tom, as he and Mike made eye contact.

The whispered decision began it all. The three found their way to Fitzy's dorm room after the meeting. Fitzy requested a single room and got one. As a large man he was very insecure of his body. When he wrestled in high school he would wear a tight tee shirt under his singlet.

Fitz, the Connecticut native, lived in the freshman dorms, which were right in the middle of campus; across the street from the athletic complex they just left. Dorm room fun supervened in the small single, as Tom and Mike journeyed into a residence hall they had never visited before. The three that were all quite different found something they all enjoyed- getting wasted. The three each sat on the futon, bed, and bean bag, talking, laughing, chugging, and arguing.

It quickly grew apparent that Mike was far different than Fitz. The New Jersey native was a quiet kid until a few drinks were ingested to enhance his confidence in his views. A conversation on the environment and the pillars of our society would run rampant. Fitzy, though, sure gave him a hard time and poured fuel on the fire. The medium build scrapper blatantly told Fitzy, "I am the true conservative, I want to conserve this earth!"

Mike took up environmental science, a subject that was dear to his heart since he was ten. Concerned with the world he lived in, Mike felt few things were left untainted by synthetic chemicals. Mike had read a great amount on the impact of mixing synthetic chemicals in organs. In Fitzy's room he told the two during his initial rant, "Yeah, maybe the test for one chemical shows minimal damage, but what if there are strands of four different chemicals all mixed together in the liver. Our bodies cannot digest or breakdown this shit."

He also shared that his independent research concluded that it would take thousands of years to understand the impact of mixing synthetic chemicals upon DNA. Tom, impressed, told Mike, "Man you gotta write a book."

Throughout high school, Mike Williams spent most of his evenings hanging out with a laptop, which seemed to be velcroed to his lap the entire evening. Research was performed toward everything he held curiosity toward through Internet searches. Furthermore, he amassed quite the library of cheap old books for an eighteen year old. If a search led him to a cheap used book on Amazon he would purchase it, but never for more than five dollars.

Fitzy quickly considered Mike as an environmental extremist. Mike told the two that he tried to eat and clean everything organically. He cleaned his room with a water vinegar solution. Mike was one of those who would complain about all the plastic and styrofoam used by the college. "That coffee cup is gonna be here for a long time boy!"

Tom held a similar interest as that of Mike. He too loved nature. Plants and trees were his main interest aside from wrestling. He had some landscaping experience from his summer job at a private high school in Windsor. Thus, a major in plants and landscape design, made the most sense. Even before he attended a college course, Tom learned nearly every variety of tree or shrub that grew in New England. He remembered most of the species each mentioned to him by his arborist boss, as well as, carrying with him a flora encyclopedia.

Grades in the first semester of freshman year reached a GPA never obtained in high school- a 3.0. Tom told his mother during their weekly phone call, "The prerequisites are very easy. I just have to show up." Wendy was thrilled.

First semester though, there would be one constant distraction at Springfield. His roommate, Nicholas Pace, a fellow-wrestling recruit from Connecticut, did not plan on wrestling. Impetus was in a far different realm than becoming an All-American. Tom's roommate experienced all the mind-altering substances available in International Hall, which would take place all hours of the day. This led Tom to witness the many dynamics of drugs. Many days, Nick would be so zapped that Tom would leave the dorm for class at nine a.m. and return at three p.m. only to find him in the exact same condition- upright in his bed with the same cd on repeat.

Tom had no interest in Nick's conduct first semester. Wrestling took precedence. Practices began in October. Tom, however, had been training since the onset of freshman year. He lifted three days a week and ran four days. Additionally, two days a week he attended open mats in the wrestling room with Mike and the rest of the motivated members of the team. The season started with the annual tournament in Ithaca. It was a great tournament that everyone could participate in, not only the varsity members. It didn't go well for Tom though- he went 0-2. Mike did very well for a freshman- he went 5-2 and placed fourth.

Tom was excited for Mike. He held no envy. As a result, their friendship would grow during the season. More or less, they were drill partners every practice. Mike wasn't one to joke around much either and Tom liked that. He was one of the few to avoid administering the big joke in the locker room of how awful New England wrestling was. Most kids in Connecticut didn't start wrestling until high school, which is very late for such a complex sport. Tom, for instance, didn't start wrestling until sophomore year. He could only precisely perform a third of the moves that Mike could. Mike had started wrestling at age five in Jersey, which was common in the powerful wrestling states.

Through a shaky freshman season in terms of performance, Tom finished the regular season with a four and twenty record. He was in and out of the starting line-up. Coach Bly made the decision that Tom would get the bid for the New England College Conference Tournament, which was the NCAA national qualifying tournament. If you win it you go to nationals. For some reason, Bly didn't want Tom to wrestle off anyone of his teammates in his weight class. The decision diminished Tom's accomplishment of making it to New England's. Tom's teammates, however, seemed fine with it- they all were inexperienced freshman as well.

Nevertheless, it was an ugly tournament. Tom won one match. Mike placed sixth- a nice accomplishment for a freshman. In a rebuilding year, with freshman making up the majority of the lineup, Springfield didn't win the New England Conference Tournament as a team for the first time in their history. A conference in which they dominated would be overtaken by Trinity College.

With the tournaments conclusion in March, the rigors of the season were done- three a.m. wake up calls, thirteen hour bus rides, bloody noses. The boys were hungry for spring semester antics.

Would temptation set in for Tom? It had for ninety-five percent of all the wrestlers who never used a substance prior to college? The parties, the girls, the booze, and the drugs were right there available to all. Hundreds upon hundreds succumbed and flunked out freshman year. Wendy was confident her son would not fall under the spell that had conquered roommate Nick, who would flunk out after freshman year.

Fortunately for Tom, he had dedicated his energy on wrestling and academics for most of freshman year. He could have two beers and then stop. However, in the spring it would quickly become blatant that Tom inherited his father's addictive personality.

All in one moment in March of spring semester 2001, accompanying Tom's vast free time, Tom changed. It was on a Thursday evening that he sat across from Nick, each on their dorm room bed listening to Nick's live Phish disc. Nick, next, got up and rearranged the exhaust fan. He then asked Tom if he wanted a rip of the substance he had never touched prior. With no hesitation, a "yes" came out of Tom's mouth. Curiosity had set in. Subsequently, Nick handed Tom his bong. Tom ripped it.

The mind would now be forever hooked.

Nights would now pass with the same casual act, some nights with others joining in. The main emphasis for Tom's daily schedule would metamorphous into getting high, rather than training and homework.

This experimentation continued for the duration of the semester. Tom didn't assume his grades or wrestling would decline with the change in focus, wherein fact his gpa would minimally decline to a 2.8 overall following finals. Fixation lied in a foreign substance Tom thought wholly beneficial.

Nick was simply the enabler. He wasn't friend material for Tom before pot. But once he sparked that bong they were best buds. Mike and Fitzy would be in

Tom and Nick's dorm room quite often getting high as well. Before Tom first smoked, however, he made an arrangement with Mike during the season that they would room together sophomore year.

Fitzy was around Tom just as often as Mike spring semester. Mike and Fitz, on the other hand, had an odd relationship. It was as if they highly respected what each other knew, but hated the way the other thought. Arguments began to emerge between the two anytime they got shitfaced together.

"Your major is a joke Fitz." Mike would say. "Politics was only created to fabricate truth. Politicians will always be in existence, because they favor the rulers and the wealthy. Policies are molded to benefit a microscopic percentage of deeply-rooted people. The truly powerful "ordinary" people who take a stand for change and overcome the impossible struggles hold no importance."

Sophomore Year

The summer in Connecticut subsequent to freshman year was quite dull compared to college. He worked at the prestigious private high school in Windsor, Loomis Chaffee, as a groundskeeper. A job he carried over from high school. The job served as a great foundation for his major, and too, it was the best means to save near fifteen hundred for the upcoming year.

The brightest spot for Tom was when the three college buds would get together for overnights. One weekend they met up in Jersey, then on another night they were in Wethersfield getting stoned, and on another occasion they were camping out on the beach. They never stayed over Fitzy's though. There was no privacy. He had four younger siblings being raised by a single mother in a small apartment in Enfield. The key for a great outing was an eighth and a thirty rack, which was always present. Fitzy had the easy pot connection in Enfield.

Tom didn't go insane from consumption the end of freshman year, but the year to follow would be an entirely different story. Mike and Tom were so pumped to be living together.

The three hung out so often freshman year, Fitzy even chose to follow them sophomore year. Home for the trio was the second floor of International Hall- Tom's second year in a row. Fitzy lived in a single room next door on the second floor. Inty hall was co-ed and it was rumored around campus as the drug dorm. Any drug could be found and purchased inside- from prescription to illegal. It seemed as the higher you went up in the elevator, the higher the shit you would find.

Any robust ideological differences didn't interfere with the friendship of the three at all. Arguments for Fitz were enjoyable. He wanted to stir anger in Mike at any opportunity. Mike, however, took everything personally. Urgency was always expressed to prove all his points. The three, however, would find something they couldn't argue about.

Sophomore year the three would discover the joy of stoned Frisbee. It was a trip to the beach the prior summer, during one of their outings, that a group of girls were throwing the biz in the sand. The social butterfly that Fitzy was led him over thirty feet to join in the circle without even asking for permission. A smile and a stretched out arm expecting a throw was all he did. Anyhow, the teenage girls threw the towering Fitzy the biz immediately. Fitzy next shouted, "Come on dudes." The two joined their large friend and the rest is history. The co-ed group of nine threw the biz for a good two hours before the three boys needed another fix back in their tent.

In the tent behind another rip, Mike said, "Man we gotta get a biz for in front of Inty!"

"Yeah Fitz," Tom said, "Nice job with the ladies."

"It would have been better if I got some numbers for tonight, but it's kind of hard when the parents are right behind you. Yeah, the green in front of Inty is ideal!"

With the completion of unpacking and setting up their rooms upon their return to Springfield, the next thing the three did was the installation of an exhaust fan in Tom and Mike's window. Fitz was the handy man, as his father. Though, Mike consistently got in his say. Next step, get high. Mike had bought a huge three foot bong for the dorm room the previous summer. It was a very pleasant surprise for the other two. Along with the bong, Mike brought a regulation sized Frisbee- a 1, 7, 5, as Fitzy called it. Paradise ensued. They would go out and play Frisbee nearly every day-rain or shine. This routine- a bong hit and then the biz- came to be a ritual for the next three years in college. Many courses were skipped in order to fulfill the routine, as the three had such different schedules. During their time throwing the biz an intriguing conversation would always arise.

Obviously, if it was Fitzy who initiated the subject matter, the topic was one related to public affairs. If Tom was talkative, his deep thoughts reflected a topic that usually had to do with either trees or some method to prevent poverty. Mike, however, would point out the evils within our environment. Energy was always a big topic. Mike knew early the necessity for a new form of energy (ethyl alcohol, solar, thermal, etc.).

In the first week back on a semi-clear afternoon, Mike asked Tom and Fitz, while immediately releasing the Frisbee toward Fitz, "You guys know what those trails in the sky are. Chemtrails I think they're called."

Tom looked up. There was no interest or urgency as to the significance planes leaving streams in the sky had. "Yeah, look at those, so many streaks," Tom replied, "They're making an x. It seems like those vapors are creating artificial clouds."

Fitzy kept quiet.

That afternoon Mike would promptly research the trails via his computer. It seemed odd to him that clouds were forming from the expansion of plane exhaust. At the moment the light bulb lit up, he shouted over to Tom, napping on the futon, "Remember Tom when I asked you, what in the world are they spraying up there? Well, it ain't no joke Tom, those are Chemtrails. Do you know why they are called that? What do you think they are comprised of? Well its metal particulates- Aluminum Oxide, Barium, Strontium, Copper Sulfate, and Potassium Iodide."

With the guidance of a search engine Mike found more and more. "Here we go, here's a website dedicated to G-e-o-e-n-g-i-neering. Apparently, chemtrails are a form of geoengineering, which became a common practice in the mid 90's. Back in the day a similar practice was called cloud seeding, which was a silver iodide application within the stratosphere, but now our solar radiation management plan uses far different chemicals."

Scrolling down on the web page, Mike said, "Wow! This shit is a globally united task man! In 1999 the U.N. issued reports entitled 'Aviation Produced Aerosols and Cloudiness,' and also, 'Modeling The Chemical Composition of The Future Atmosphere.'

Reading while scrolling down, Mike shared, "The UK Royal Society published a report that took interest in a wide range of various particles that could be released into the stratosphere with the objective of scattering sunlight back into space."[i]

"We're being forced to breath in and ingest this shit. We have no right to natural oxygen now! Talk about civil rights. They say it improves global warming, that it reflects the sun's rays back to the atmosphere before they reach earth. Bullshit, that aerosol smokescreen is trapping the heat. Asbestos was once a great idea too, and now look at what it has left behind. I never thought I'd be saying this but their trying to control the weather."

"Weather has now become viewed as a method of stealth warfare. There is a government publication released in '96 that determines control of the weather could possibly occur by the year 2025. Thus, negative food production through unfavorable conditions, positive weather conditions for corporate interest, population distress, removal from certain territories, would all be possible. See right here."

Mike pointed his right index finger toward his laptop. "'Owning the Weather by 2025' was disclosed in August 1996. They're trying to have control over mother freakin nature and only certain corporations will benefit, not the petty American citizen who funds the salary of the men making decisions on behalf of the corporations. As far back as 1957, the president's advisors on weather understood that the military may have an unlimited prospect within weather modification. But consider this Tom, if all this shit their spraying gets in our water, our plants, and our oxygen, the three most important elements necessary for our survival, this shit could be much more lethal a weapon than the atomic bomb. Did we know the risks before we started this spraying?"

"Why is it so secret Mike?" Tom asked.

"No idea. And I don't even know the beginning of what these chemicals do to the weather patterns. Does it alter high or low pressure."

Tom was taken aback and felt betrayed. He did not like secrets. He had to keep one inside his entire life so he wouldn't be made a fool. For Tom, if things are kept secret or manipulated, they were not going to turn out well. It wouldn't be natural. When all this was brought to Fitzy's attention that evening, he just shook it off just as he did with all of Mike's environmental talks. "EPA needs to mind their business," was his usual response.

To Fitz, Mike was also strange in the sense that he was a vegetarian, all because, as Mike would say, "humans aren't supposed to consume mass amounts of meat".

Tom, in fact, was Mike's leading adversary in the meat debate. He told Mike, "I think meat, eggs, and cheese are very beneficial, especially for the brain. See Mike, there are good cholesterols out there. I learned in science that a quarter of our brain is made out of a form of cholesterol. The human mind is incomparable to that of animals who eat plants every day."

Beginning sophomore year, Mike would become aware of a natural mind altering substance. That October, a popular drug became available during fall foliage time at Springfield. One of Tom's classmates, Ted, from the plant anatomy course, brought to Tom's attention that he picked up a lot of boomers back home in Rhode Island.

"What the hell is a boomer?" Tom asked.

Shrooms, man.

Mushrooms?

Yeah man, want to lose your mind? Ted asked.

Tom brought the news back to Mike and Fitzy on floor two. The proposition was welcomed with open mouths, but the three would quickly renege within one conversation.

At this point in time the two wrestlers had not conceived they would receive any ill effects from the daily sessions upon their wrestling performance.

Before wrestling tournament season began in November a much more important sport would begin for Mike and Tom- Ultimate Frisbee. The ritual for the three, in its early September days, would quickly gain multiple interested peers, who enjoyed the exact same habits. The first two to join in with the original three were Chris Moy, a Chinese student very talented in Frisbee, and Kyle Fogg, an extremely talented thrower.

Rail skinny, with a concrete spiked brown receding hairline, Kyle could throw the Frisbee by any method flawlessly. He was quickly coined by Fitzy "The Glow Stick Ninja" for his nightly escapades through the dorms rolling on ecstasy. Two girls would join in around the same time, Haley and Spring, two athletic soccer players who could catch anything. With the group expanding, Kyle, who was familiar with Ultimate Frisbee prior, brought up the idea of trying a pick-up game. Sure enough, the crew had the time of their life.

Games continued throughout the fall. Multiple wrestling teammates would join in on the second floor for a session and then partake in a game. Just as talent was developing with the biz, Fitzy discovered there was an intramural ultimate Frisbee league played on the artificial turf football field behind the townhouses. It was too late to sign up, but there was another season in the spring. On cool fall nights every once in awhile, the three would get ripped and check out games on the bleachers.

The Frisbee spawned many new friendships. Kyle Fogg was a twisted dude from California. There was a rumor he was bisexual, which didn't bother anyone. He knew all the secret spots on campus, which he shared with the three. The favorite for everyone that had come in and out of Springfield was the railway bridge above Lake Massasoit, which could only be reached by climbing above the rusty fifteen-foot Iron Gate. The gate, however, served no purpose. Gangs of students, athletic or not, easily scaled the sturdy structure, which sat on the tracks, bordered by flora. Sunsets reflecting off the water were magnificent.

Amid all this bliss, however, the day came.

The morning of 9/11, the usual three sat in Tom and Mike's dorm room watching Fitzy's favorite propaganda news channel as they had every morning. It was far past dawn, just as any other morning, when breaking news came upon the cable news station. "A plane has flown into a tower!"

Thus, enduring the breaking news of the worse foreign invasion their country had ever seen was in full swing. Things now had changed forever. Reliving youth in college subsequent to a dark childhood was happening at nineteen for Tom, but this halted euphoria. The pain Robert had permanently forced into Tom had been revisited.

The attack, considered that of terrorism, was an act unfamiliar to any young man throughout the country. Thousands of innocent men, women, and children of all walks of lives perished.

'The Truth News Channel', which was on the majority of time in Tom's dorm room, aside from evening sporting events, provided the half-truths that molded Fitzy's ideology. Fitzy, by any means, had control of the remote at all times, even though it was not his room. Many a wrestling matches took place for that remote. The three were pretty equal, even with Fitzy considerably heavier. He did nonetheless live next door. The large framed young man was in Tom's room more often than Tom.

Tom's cubed dorm room was small in size, but he and Mike made the most out of it. They were able to fit two futons and two beds in the minimal dorm room. Before they moved in together, Mike had his father, a carpenter, build stilts for the two single metal bed frames, which raised the beds an additional six feet. Hence, each young man was able to fit their own futon under each loft. The walls were covered with tapestries, a Marley poster, and other herbal innuendos. The room also consistently smelled of nag chamba incense. At certain times they were able to fit near ten people in the room. Maximum capacity would be reached when the window fan would be flipped around in order to serve as an exhaust, while the bubbler would be passed to the left.

Conversation, no matter who was present, would unfold into one filled with popular legislation, in which Fitzy's projected assumptions were always in the right. Taxes, immigration, education, welfare, health care, war, environment; you name it, Fitzy held a domineering argument.

Tom, in fact, was annoyed deep down by Fitzy. Many winter nights after wrestling practice he would walk into his empty room with the 'The Truth News' broadcasting. Also, some nights Fitzy would sleep over on the futon with the channel blasting, but Tom would never say a word. To Tom it seemed that that channel was promoting a certain way for him to think- opinion rather than fact- which conveyed a message that did not seem just, truthful, or proper; it spawned anger and hatred!

There was no difference in opinion on the morning of September 11th as to what had been expressed on the television. As the three watched silently, listening to every word of speculation, the second plane flew into the second tower. "What the fuck is going on?" Tom asked.

"It's the fucking Russians!" Fitzy said, "The cold war ain't over."

"No, it's an inside job," Mike said, "do you know how many times we have antagonized war under false pretense? Fitzy, how can you make up some random accusation without facts? That's what's wrong with this country. Anyone can speculate about some make believe story and make people think it is reality! Plain and simple: AMERICA'S MOST LUCRITIVE BUSINESS IS WAR!"

"Chill out Mike, I'm just saying. Make's me think about the cold war." Fitzy didn't take his opinion any further into his familiar spat at such a point in time.

"Communism, terrorism, toryism! They're all scapegoats for us to administer our skewed self-aggrandizing agenda under the pretense of promoting national security. See Fitzy, as jury, judge, and executioner, we receive the secret prize from whichever country we invade. The only responsibility we must fulfill in order to reap what we sow is to create the war hysteria!" Mike was now standing and yelling in front of the television with an erect wingspan.

"Calm down, think of what has just happened, who knows how many people have died! ... What's going to happen next? Why would anyone hate us so much?" Tom said.

No other news channel coverage was appropriate for Fitzy's viewing particularly on this morning. He denied Mike's request to "change this bullshit." The conservative was especially fond of a male anchor named Richard Cotter, who was the face of "The Truth News Channel". The white forty-five year-old anchor, with a side part of his dyed brown hair, expressed his extreme views daily. Did he really hold these feelings? Or was it just an act?

Arguments were constant on Cotter's evening show "The American Mind," which aired at eight PM, but as was the case with all severe tragedies and breaking news, Cotter was on air immediately following the first attack.

Every squabble between Fitz and Mike that spawned from the topics made Tom quite uneasy- a characteristic that was shaped when he was a little boy. He stood clear of making any comment. For some reason, he was one to take into account both perspectives- pros and cons.

'Truth News' anchor Cotter, on the other hand, held concrete views, most of which favored warfare and satire. To Tom, the "The Truth News" was no more than a profit driven news station that promoted rumors, misinformation, half-truths, and speculative deception on foreign nations. For war to be successful, Tom had known inside, the media must be one of the first conspirators. More or less, intuition spoke that journalism had become a weapon to spread terror just as a bomb would. If fear sways peoples emotions and decisions then why not use it to promote a governments agenda?

Sure enough, Richard Cotter appeared on air the moment following the 'breaking news' bulletin. The three were in the room around 9:30 prior to their first classes- they wisely chose to have later classes in acknowledgment of their sleeping patterns freshman year.

Cotter read off the teleprompter:

"Today's horrific spectacle is an event that will forever be underscored in our history. Yes two planes have attacked us. With the two towers set ablaze, desperation has now forced people to jump out of buildings to avoid incineration. Planes have destroyed the Twin Towers. There are reports coming in that this is a planned invasion, a blatant attack on our freedom!"

"This is a grave day for our freedom and national security. Be prepared, we are now in a state of war. Justice must prevail."

What great confusion upon Tom's sensitive, fragile, mind. From the futon evaporated a stunned silence. The young men watched the buildings, trophies for universal relations, blown up repeatedly from alternate angles. Depression and the odd feeling that death presents cowed Tom. Subsequent to the Mike and Fitz verbal tirade, the three didn't speak for minutes aside from a quick curse word based on shock. "Oh shit."

The site of the burning building would replay over in all their minds as it had on the TV. So many innocent people perished. Nothing could be done to help the victims. As a small boy he held a dream to make peace in the world, but never could discover how. He, lethargically, portrayed a common persona, which was not portrayed on "The Truth News".

Victory in this conflict was not going to be achieved fictionally by action figures or video games. Sorrow could not be shook off, nor could Tom help in any way. Happiness, hope, and love, were all sought after, but most importantly, was the truth sought as well?

Mike didn't know what to think- he was the conspiracy theory guy. He felt he had quite a grasp on reality, which was discussed at all times with Tom. Mike spooked Tom often with his knowledge of the synthetic reality. The first time Mike saw what his roommate used to brush his teeth with, he yelled, "That shit has fluoride in it you fool!"

Environmental issues were always going to be the fuel for Mike's fire. Self-education unearthed that fluoride was used in sections of New York and New Jersey's drinking water. School wasn't teaching any of this.

Subsequent to Tom rinsing out his mouth, Mike shared his research, "How could something that enhances bad traits in other chemicals, and is used to produce high octane fuel be healthy to ingest? Huge industry money backs the pro-fluoride scientists. Our use of fluoride is all the result of who held power during the industrial boom. See, fluoride use by dentists is a smokescreen for the disposal of factory fluoride waste. Little attention has been placed on the pollution and harm on the human body fluoride causes. Over exposure is called fluorosis, which has a debilitating effect on the skeletal structure."

"We rid big factories of their poison and then flavor it and give it to our kids. Fluosilicic acid, for instance, is removed from smokestacks of phosphate fertilizer mills, so the fluoride does not become airborne to affect livestock and plants. It then is sold to towns and cities. The fluoride is then shipped out in rubber tanks and then mixed in with drinking water. The phosphate companies are then spared an extreme toxic waste disposal fee. What a great deal!"

"America for some reason did not want to read the fine print for fluoride. Rather than listen to the European scientists in the 1930's, who claimed fluoride was very harmful and responsible for many illnesses, America chose to use fluoride to enrich uranium for nuclear weapons, and then, dump it in the public water supply. The key for fluoride to be celebrated in our society was the promotion of its positive public image by the military and profit based researchers. It appeared to make teeth white, so it was a go."[ii]

Tom replied, "Maybe they put just enough in so it works properly?"

"Tom, it's in the water we drink. Our bodies are made out of pure H2O. Not Fluorine!"

The two talked late into the night nearly every occasion Fitzy wasn't underneath the two elevated in their beds. The conversations were disturbing, but therapeutic for Tom. Without Fitzy around Mike could share his angle without interruption.

One night after 9/11, about twelve thirty, Mike shouted out across the room to Tom, "We are so far from reality Tom! I'll tell you what's truly happening, we are near the final days of high quantity oil production. What would happen if gas and oil were just not available any longer? Yes, the age of oil will soon become a part of our history, and it will be our hands that remove the final drips when the pipes run dry. My prediction is, as World War I came to fruition because of the desire for the vast pools of oil by Britain and Germany (to name a few countries), World War III will unfold as the greed increases for the final drops of oil."

"Accordingly, our intention is to use military force in order to gain control of the remaining oil rich regions. Why, because it favors our national security. The strategy for our national security is quite simple: in order to produce a preemptive war we must first present a foreign nation as a great evil power."

"My ethics teacher had shared with the class a memo written on September 9th, 2001 received by the Cabinet Office of British Prime Minister Tony Blair."

Mike jumped off his bed, turned on the small lamp, and ravaged through his miniature filing cabinet. "Here it is!"

Submission to the Cabinet Office on Energy Policy

The world faces severe hydrocarbon supply difficulties. Global oil supply is currently at political risk ... Large investments in Middle East production, if they occur, could raise output, but only to a limited extent. The main exception is Iraq. ... The global output of conventional oil will soon decline. The date of the peak depends on the size of Middle East reserves.

"We know this! But our public servants keep it a big secret. Why? Why aren't our paid servants preparing us for a future without oil consumption? Everything is petroleum based, why are we not changing over?"

"The very men at the genesis of our policies have dictated what the necessity for our national security should be. Many of these men no doubt have had their interests in oil or law for many years before they entered the public service. 'Only the administration's good friends within the oil industry would get lucrative contracts. Cheney's Haliburton Corp. was at the top of the list, along with U.S. and British oil companies.'[iii] Therefore, if previous interest was for their own private benefit, do you think their decisions had changed with an increase in power? All this talk of Iraq, Cheney's Haliburton had the Iraqi oil fields mapped out in 1999. Cheney's former private corporations were prepared to provide the needs for 100,000 troops deployed in the Middle East."

"Documents published in the late 90's reveal that both top financial factions and future Bush cabinet members pleaded for an invasion of the Middle East by means of the American military. A change in the American society was also seen as a necessity. An American metamorphous was to be produced subsequent to a future attack. Thus, following 9/11, the threat of terror brought about mass hysteria upon an injured people, which was to be fueled exclusively by the Bush Intelligence Community. Furthermore, the six media conglomerates provided unsourced and misleading propaganda.

"So, if our President is breaking laws, but makes the comment, 'You are either with us or against us', where does that leave a morally conscience citizen?"

"You want to know when this shit started going down Tom? It was under President Reagan when a secretive intelligence community took control of the nation away from the President- Reagan didn't even know what was going down under his watch. He was an actor- a man that had the ability to make the most horrific American acts seem magnificent. He had the presidency taken over by his very own former CIA Director vice president."

"All facts show this mess has been formulated by Sr. and his associates- corporations and policy makers thinking they can take the strongest nation hostage and make it perform ill natured acts in the name of the people they support and represent. What has truly transpired is that a secretive intelligence community has taken over control of the government in order to only benefit the greedy. As long as cheap oil is available we will make no progress!"

"What if a nation commits horrific secret acts, but is still portrayed to be a nation that can do no wrong?" Mike closed the night, "People keep secrets to feel superior and remain powerful- that's all it is."[iv]

And so, the great disorder amassed through the difficult childhood now appeared again with the attack on his homeland. Tom did not know how to look inside to understand his emotions. He hid them. Perception made his conduct appropriate. Alongside Mike and Fitzy, Tom was living in paradise- high every day, no worries. College was no more than the most effective way to hide unemployment. It became a life without worry, because he buried the worry. No attention was ever put toward life after college, while attending college.

Obviously, drugs were largely responsible for the euphoria in a volatile world. And the drugs too were used every day during wrestling season.

Sophomore wrestling season was a rollercoaster ride for Tom in terms of performance and conduct. Coach Bly first opened the preseason meeting, "I am not looking back at the past season. We were young, this year is going to be different, we have much more experience. I have changed up the schedule and have a surprise to announce."

"This season we will be attending the Sunshine Duals in Florida. We will fly down December 26th and wrestle in the two day tournament on the 28th and 29th.

We will then spend New Years Eve and New Years day down there. The tournament is right next to Universal Drive at the Orange County Convention Center. The only cost you will need to cover is for recreation."

"Yeah Coach!" hummed from the group sitting Indian style.

The season started well in Ithaca. Tom went 2-2, much better than the previous season, but he didn't place. Mike placed fourth, not too shabby again. There were two nationally ranked kids in his 149 lb. weight class.

Of course, weed was carried on the twelve hour bus ride and into the hotel. Mike and Tom would not tell anyone else though- they would simply go for a walk outside the hotel to find a good isolated spot. Once found, they sparked up behind the hemlock border. No one knew.

With a highly favorable third place team finish at the opening tournament in Ithaca, New England dual meets would follow. This year, in contrast to the previous season, matches went well for the team. They beat Trinity 22-9 in team points, the reigning New England College Conference Champions. This dual meet hosted the most important match for Tom in the early sophomore season. He faced off against the number one ranked wrestler in the conference at 157 lb.

Tom won. He wrestled smart and capitalized on the lone mistake his opponent made. His mother also came to the match in Hartford. She was ecstatic with the results. She had no idea how good he had gotten through wrestling talented teammates every day. Then again, she had no clue he was constantly impaired while achieving such an improvement.

Victories accumulated through the freezing winter months. The time would quickly come for Florida! A buzz was shared by the entire team. Not only were they participating in a tournament with top ten nationally ranked teams, but they were spending New Years Eve on Universal Drive. It couldn't get much better.

At Bradley International airport everything went smooth for the entire college team to depart. Arriving in warm Florida was a breath of fresh air for everyone. Mike, Tom, and a handful of others were goofing around on the flat escalator, walking against it. A carefree attitude was held going into such a talented tournament.

The tournament, however, went awful. They faced off first against the number one team in the nation, Augsburg. Springfield didn't win one individual match. Not a match was close. Bly was pissed at the effort- "No Fucking Intensity!" The next match was against sixth ranked College of New Jersey. It was close but they lost 18-14. Tom and Mike both went 0-2. That was the tournament for Springfield. It was a double elimination team tournament. The last thing Bly said to the team at the convention center before they left for the hotel was, "None of you better mess up anymore down here."

New Years Eve came, what else were college students going to do. Tom and Mike had an upper classmen by two thirty packs for them, which they dumped in the tub with ice. Thus, their room became the hangout for the younger wrestlers on the team-freshman and sophomores. The cooler older guys peeked in.

Around nine o'clock there was eight consistently in the room getting bombed. "Dude did you see those golf carts when we came in," said Alex, a mulatto freshman from New York. "The keys were right in them."

"Really," Mike said.

"Let's go for a ride," Jeremy, another freshman, chimed in.

"We're paying for the hotel, we can use them," Alex said.

"I'm in," was recited by Alex, Mike, Jeremy, Brett, Justin, and finally Tom. Yes, six drunk underaged college athletes had the audacity to fill a small golf cart parked in front of the hotel, and turn the key as if they owned it. Alex was the first to sit in the drivers seat. The second he turned the key they were off. Mike and Tom held on for dear life. The two stood on the back bumper while holding onto the side roof support. The other four squeezed in the four seats. About a mile down, passing all the lights and themes, Alex turned around in a different hotel's parking lot and drove back to their hotel. They were yelling at people walking by while laughing the entire ride. Upon return, Alex then drove the cart fully loaded through the double doors of the side entrance, into the hotel with no hesitation . Mike jumped off pushed up on the elevator control panel, "Let's bring it up!"

The door opened and Justin said, "It ain't going to fit dumbass."

Mike hopped back on. "Let's get out of here."

A second tour down Universal Drive transpired. However, the hotel security guards, from the hotel the wrestlers turned around in, saw the stolen cart. Security thought the cart was its own. On this second tour, the white security van performed a u-turn and then started racing down the strip. In thirty seconds they reached the unusual method for transportation on the strip. Next, security pulled alongside the golf cart. "Pull over now," yelled an obese white male in a security uniform.

"Aw shit we're caught," said Alex.

They all knew they were done. Tom was the only one who would politely and truthfully answer the security guards questions. With all the answers security contacted the wrestlers' hotel and the police. He was told to bring the six student athletes back to the hotel.

The instant they walked into the lobby, Coach Bly was waiting. "Boy, you guys fucked up! Get out of my sight now!"

The six hustled into the elevator. As the door shut they all began to chuckle. "Wow, I don't think anything is going to happen to us," said Alex.

"It's not like we did anything wrong, we were going to return it. That's why its here," said Mike.

An hour later, an hour before midnight, every wrestler involved is startled by a large pound upon their doors. It was the Orange County Sherriff, along with Coach Bly. The six formed a half circle around the Sherriff and Bly. "Listen here," said the Sherriff, "you boys fucked up. The hotel don't want you here... Your coach don't want you here either. No charges are going to be filed, but you better get the hell out of Orange County right now. Never come back until I forget about this."

With that, Coach Bly said, "Get your shit, I'm taking you to the airport."

The six gathered their belongings and met Bly in the van rental. The only thing said the entire ride to the airport was by their coach, "I notified your parents, they are aware of the circumstances, and that you will be spending New Years Day at the airport finding a flight home in exchange for your other ticket."

Thus, the six sat in the airport New Years day until three in the afternoon when a flight had six openings to Hartford. Tom was not thrilled. He knew his mother knew everything that happened. Drinking was involved. He did call her before they boarded. "Mom you heard?"

"Yes, I'm very pissed at you right now."

"I messed up."

"You sure did. How are you boys going to get back to school," she asked.

"Can you pick us up?"

"Sure."

They arrived at Bradley Airport at seven o' clock and made it back to Springfield before eight. Wendy didn't seem overly concerned after she heard the story shared in pieces by each participant. It became a big joke. Wendy, nevertheless, kept her stern facade. "I know you boys are young and are going to do silly things, but please try to control your actions if you're drinking. Don't drive! Tom I'll talk to you about this later."

The topic was never discussed between the two. Separation was setting in. The freshman weekly phone calls became monthly.

They were back at practice two days later, subsequent to a harsh meeting filled with warnings if a similar act was to occur again with the six. A meeting Tom and Mike were stoned at. Back on the practice mat it was the usual routine. Tom was now ranked one in the conference, but even that didn't increase his drive or desire to improve into a higher echelon.

Stupidity had sure set in. Tom and Mike decided to go out in long sleeve tees and shorts, and have a Frisbee toss in a February snowstorm- a week before the New England Conference Tournament. If number one seed Tom won, he would qualify for the NCAA National Tournament, similar to the NCAA basketball tournament.

Accordingly, Tom got sick- real sick. Bronchitis was the prognosis at the health center. He was put on antibiotics. He still wanted to wrestle even though he was twenty percent. Tom didn't realize, as the number one seed, everyone was coming at him.

He somehow won his first match against a week opponent from Norwich University. The next match he wrestled against was a strong Coast Guard opponent. It was the most painful match he ever faced. When the whistle blew to begin the match he appeared as a skilled wrestler, but as soon as the whistle blew for a match break, he was hunched over hacking up a lung, barely making it back to the center of the mat. Somehow he won 3-1 getting one take down through every ounce of energy.

With two wins, he was now in the semifinals. One win away from the finals. He would have to face the same Trinity College kid he defeated earlier. The results this time would be far different. Tom could barely move his hand up to shake his opponent's hand, which was done prior to the match starting. Weakness was obvious. Fifteen seconds in Tom got launched right to his back and pinned without a fight. He was done for the tournament; he couldn't wrestle back for third. Even though he forfeited his remaining matches, team points were scored by Tom. He placed sixth, all because he reached the semifinals.

Mike took third while the team finished first. It was a much better season for Coach Bly. He never did mention the golf cart incident again.

Life after wrestling began yet again. Warm sunny March days signaled the return of the ritual. The crew had largely expanded. Many of the freshman wrestlers who highly regarded Tom and Mike wanted to join them in everything they did. And what did they do most? Toss the biz. Kyle Fogg, Moy, and the girls were still on board. Alex the golf cart thief joined the crew along with Justin another Orange County offender. At times there were ten against ten games in front of Inty. One early April day filled with clouds a slender kid stopped over to talk with the group that was sitting huffing and puffing after an intense ultimate game.

"What's up guys," said the stranger.

"Howdy, hey, sup man," replied the gang.

"You guys get some serious games in. My name is Chowski, its what all my friends call me back home," said the young man whose face resembled a sly fox.

"Hey Chowski," said Tom.

"Mind if I join in one day."

"Please anytime," Fitzy chimed in.

"You guys gonna sign up for the season, I'm looking for a team, and there's only a week for sign ups."

"Oh shit, I was oblivious," said Mike, "Yeah I'll go over and sign up at the community center tomorrow. I think we need a team name though."

"I always liked the name Jerrytown," said Chowski, "honor the great one, you know."

"Dude you're in," said Mike, "I take it you blaze."

"Oh yes, session on the bridge in ten, I'll match." Chowski, with his purple bandana on, turned and ran to the neighboring Abbey Hall to pick up his stash. No one had any clue who this Chowski was. It seemed as if he were a hermit who only came out of his dorm to play Frisbee or smoke on the bridge.

In total fifteen people climbed over the gate to become elevated. Three blunts were rolled. Hence, a new friend with many similarities was made in Chowski. And he didn't give a shit about anything.

Thus Jerrytown was formed. There were more than enough players to fulfill the requirements for a co-ed intramural team- seven players on the field at a time- five boys, two girls. The four initial girls were real good, too!

In the first intramural season there was not one close game. The team of twelve was ripped, shitfaced, rolling face, each game. Players on the other team would complain to the intramural officials on hand that the other players were stoned, but all the officials could say in response was, "We can't drug test them."

Chowski was a rebel. He would smoke butts right on the artificial turf field. One game he was told to put it out, wherein he responded "Eat my ass with a spoon." All to the chagrin of the official, who let him finish his butt. First J town season success- Intramural Ultimate Frisbee Champions!

School ended for the summer. The three did the usual summer duties, while making time every other weekend to get together for campouts.

Junior Year

Similar to sophomore year, Fitzy, Tom, and Mike played a lot of Frisbee and did a lot of drugs to begin the school year. No sooner than one step into Mike and Tom's dorm room, a heady skunk scent would consistently present itself.

Early on junior year, the entrance into bars was a little tricky. The three were still minors. Fake ID's were provided from older teammates on the wrestling team. Tom received his from Billy Donner. It looked similar enough to the twenty year old that he never had a problem. Mike's ID didn't look much like him, the photo was of someone with blonde hair, he had dark brown hair. Nevertheless, he was only denied once from the various downtown Springfield bars. They couldn't be denied; they wanted to join in on the college nightlife. Tom was always a bit hesitant to use it. Yet as soon as Mike, Fitzy, and Tom threw a couple down the pallet in the dorms nothing would stop them from getting in the bar or club. They always had a great time out.

Mike and Tom held repute as roughnecks, guys not to mess with, but it wasn't because they performed any massive bar fight to merit it. Their intimidating stature was all stirred because they wrestled. Everyone on campus feared the wrestling team. Rumors of past fisticuffs ran rampant. The football team was very weak, so the male population felt the wrestling community were the most dominant meatheads. The next in line were the gangly awkward volleyball team.

The wrestlers had never lost one fight ever. They swarmed like bees protecting a hive. Mike and Tom, however, never got in a fight at Springfield College-passive stoners, never putting themselves in a scuffle.

The younger kids, on the other hand, always felt they had to prove themselves to the upper classmen. On several occasions Tom had to break up bar fights spawned by the underclassmen too with fake id's.

It was usually the same three who somehow individually scored the days entertainment each day for the entire year- either a bag or a bottle, albeit there was someone else now always present during the session. Chowski, wrestlers, hippies, mystics, jocks, all stopped by daily.

The three did all have small petty summer jobs, which provided money up until the end of first semester. Bars, late night munchies, write ups, and herb, would all lead to calls home for money. One write up alone cost Tom two hundred dollars the first week, all because he was too lazy to flip the fan around in the window. Resident assistant (RA) rounds always seemed to follow once the pipe was lit during the late night session. Tom would take full blame, even though Mike joined in.

Jerrytown, nonetheless, was back and stronger than ever. It seemed each year existing J-town players would connect with the unknown fellow dirty hippies on campus. A common connection brought new members of JerryTown aboard the train.

There were more than a few new members on board for the fall intramural season, especially a couple very talented girls, Jacky and Joleen. This season, however, a new team would enter the intramural league that was good- very good. It was a collection of cross country kids, tall lanky volleyball kids, and swimmers that made up "The Crusaders". This hybrid team of well conditioned athletes formed together with the sole intention to dethrone Jerrytown.

Jtown's inaugural season brought opponents together from various teams into one, all who had their feather's ruffled and wanted revenge.

Not one other team could touch either Jerrytown or The Crusaders in the league. But when the two clashed it was epic. The first game was ugly, it was super windy, but more influential was the fact that more than half of Jerrytown was shitfaced from playing beer dye for three hours prior to the game. Tom was the sloppiest. And as the touchdown maker, or yellow lab as Fitzy called Tom, was not a factor, Jerrytown lost. The height and reach of the volleyball players was too much in the windy conditions. The wrestlers were never out worked, but in this game they were out skilled. Chowski got some good one liner's in towards the goofiest members of The Crusaders. One classic nickname Chowski dished out toward a tall annoying volleyball player was 'Vegetable Lasagna,' whatever that meant.

After the game everyone was riled up. Chowski told every one to jump on the roof of his Oldsmobile, which only Fitzy, Mike, and Tom did, Chowski then put it in reverse, and drove all the way back to Inty Hall backwards through the public roads within campus.

That boy was fortunate not to be caught. Nevertheless, it was blackout central back on the second floor.

The loss set up the most amazing intramural ultimate Frisbee championship game in the history of mankind. Jerrytown kept it real and didn't get too messed up for this one , with the exception of Chowski. Everyone kept to their vices. Every throw was contested, every catch dropped by a player was greeted by angry teammates. Chowski was playing very physical. Confrontation arose between Chowski and a swimmer after Chowki slid into the opponents shins. "Come on pussy, look who my teammates are! Wanna go tit for tat fool!"

The score would be tied at five by the end of regulation. First team to score in overtime on this beautiful clear October night in Springfield would claim victor. Near about two minutes into overtime an errant pass was made by The Crusaders that landed within the midfield circle. Fitzy ran over picked it up. All he did was glance over at Tom who glanced back standing on the left hash marks of the thirty yard line. He then made a full sprint toward the right corner of the endzone- a diagonal beam. Fitzy bent it like Beckham into an area no one but Tom could reach. Tom reached up dragged his two feet inside the endzone, which caused him to fall face first. The Frisbee in his right hand braced his standup. "Two feet in motherfucker!" Tom screamed as he spiked the Frisbee a foot in front of Vegetable Lasagna. Jerrytown all formed around Tom in order to celebrate utter bliss. Again, blackouts ensued for nearly the entire team inside Tom and Mike's overcrowded room.

Jerrytown was now two for two in championship games. Wrestling was quickly approaching at this time, but Tom did not care. He no longer trained in the preseason, while he was on the brink of academic ineligibility. Two weeks before wrestling started mushrooms again made their way onto campus, which was disclosed by Chowski. Mike was one of the first in line at the dealer's third floor door. Tom, Fitz, and Mike wanted a new experience rather than just smoking on the bridge.

Chowski told the three that he felt hallucinating from mushrooms opened his third eye- it made his spirit aware of another realm.

Thus, in the fall of 2002 Fitz, Tom, and Mike were introduced to mushrooms. Chowski brought over a great big bag full of the drug on a Friday night. On the futon beneath his bed, Mike held up the Ziploc bag two inches from his face. He told Tom that he would do a little research before they ingested any. It was clear, as everything else had been that Tom was going to do whatever Mike did. Come to find out, Mike discovered that Mushrooms held a plant alkaloid called Psilocybin within, which had domineering spiritual effects that stimulated the pineal gland. Mushrooms had been used in ancient times for religious rites. He read that it was best to be taken outdoors and that it could be the most spiritual experience of their life. They decided to wait until Saturday.

As Saturday morning came, Mike, Fitz, and Tom brainstormed a plan for their mushroom trip. Fitzy had slept over on the futon. With his new found knowledge of the drug, Mike decided the three should go camping. It would be the perfect outdoor setting. Massachusetts was filled with loads of natural landscape treasures.

The three agreed it would be a great experience. Tom grabbed his four person tent that was stuffed away in the furthest spot behind all the clutter under the futon. They were all packed in no time Saturday morning. Cooler of beer, bag of bud, bag of mushrooms, and one change of clothes. They picked up kielbasa, cheese, chips, ice, and water on the way with Mike's father's gas card.

An hour and a half later around two they reached a desolate State Park Campground near Pittsfield on the Appalachian Trail. They set up a temporary home and started a fire. Throwing down the thirty pack immediately ensued. There was no mention of what they were all thinking for the first couple hours until six. At this point they were feeling a good buzz as the sun began its descent. Fitzy said, "It's about that time boys. Ready to get lost."

"I am if you are." Tom looked at Mike.

"Let's do it," Mike said.

Fitzy opened the bag. Next, the caps and stems were equally divided three ways on the cooler. All three said cheers and started to eat.

The taste was poor, almost that of eating cardboard soil. They continued to pop open beers to wash the taste down. "Not the best tasting thing out there," noted Tom.

"Just wait, we ate a lot!" Fitzy said.

Half hour passed and Mike declared, "I don't feel nothing. You guys?"

"Na," replied the other two.

"I feel like I gotta move. Let's go for a hike. That steep pitch looks as good as any to see the sunset," Mike said.

"Sure," said Tom, "I feel like moving too."

The three were becoming very comfortable. Not one other soul was in the state park. The three began up the steep mountain, which bordered their campsite. Not once did the thought of getting lost in the dark, subsequent to the beautiful sunset, play a factor.

The three set out with beers held tight. Only Fitzy had a flashlight in his other hand. Mike picked up a walking stick. By the time they made it to the top the sun was nearly gone, aside from an orange sliver. In an instant, for the three it was pure darkness at the top with the exception of what little Fitzy provided. The moon's brightness too was hiding behind clouds. "Man I'm really starting to feel it," Tom said.

"Yeah, this is the potent stuff," Mike quickly responded.

On the way down, Fitzy was ahead of the two, standing one foot in front of a pine analyzing its bark. It was the longest span of silence ever to befall upon Fitz with others taking up conversation. All of a sudden Mike started to sprint down the hill. "Dude," was the only thing a disoriented Fitzy was able to slowly mumble as Mike swept past him.

Sure enough Tom followed suit. Mike was bobbing and weaving pine trees, hickories, and scattered saplings, the size of which his hands could wrap around. Tom picked up the pace to catch up. Unluckily, it was very dark and Tom held no flashlight to guide his footsteps. Bare roots were crawling between the crevasses on the mountain of rock. Just where the cliff made its greatest descent had Tom's foot met a root. At the speed he was travelling he would plummet into a nose-dive position.

Thud!

Tom did a direct face plant into the nose of a stone face. Legs flopped over his limp body. Fitzy had caught up by this time.

"Mike! I think Tom just ate it." Fitzy yelled with no other detail.

Mike hurried up from twenty-four feet away. "What, where'd he go." He approached and looked up.

All of a sudden Tom returned to his feet in an instant. There was no hesitation, just a thoughtless leap to his feet. Fitzy shined the light on Tom's face. There was a lot of blood, but no structure damage. Fitzy's eyes had doubled in size by this point on the trip. Light continued on Tom's forehead. Away an arm's length, Fitzy diagnosed the wounds. There were two significant cuts. One was located on the middle of Tom's forehead, while the other wound was located right between the eyes. "Dude I can see your brain," Fitzy said.

"Am I dead, am I going to die?" Tom cried.

"You're fine." There was no panic in Mike, he was loving life. "You need some stitches. We'll pack up and get you to the hospital."

"Man, everything just flashed." Tom seemed stunned. "I saw everything that I know in like one second."

"Let's head down," Mike said.

Sure enough they followed everything Mike prescribed. They packed up swiftly while Tom panicked minimally, pressing his bloodied white shirt upon his wounds. Mike drove Tom's red truck and they made it to the hospital within forty minutes. Tom received a total of twenty-five stitches.

When the three returned to the dorm late Saturday everyone was just getting home from the bars. Indeed, as the three walked in the entrance of Inty hall, the drunks swarmed seeking the story behind Tom's appearance. There was one girl standing outside the entrance with her girlfriend that Tom took a long glance at. He had seen her around, but up close he saw how magnificent she was.

Tom's shirt was still covered in blood. His face was swollen. He resembled the lion from The Wizard of Oz. The legend of the fall on mushrooms will live forever at Springfield College. Conversely, no one changed their habits after a severe wake up call. The fall actually promoted anarchy. They would now seek out opportunities to get wasted in order to commit the most stupid of acts.

The wrestling team thought Tom's fall was the coolest thing ever. At least once a week at practice the story would come up. It was so relevant for everyone. Eighty percent of the team was now coming stoned to practice everyday. Junior year was a standstill for Tom and Mike's performance. No improvement was made on the mat. Tom took third, while Mike took fourth in the conference tournament. The team, however, did win again.

Jerrytown would prevail in the spring as well. The Crusaders lost a couple crucial volleyballer's. Dissension arose among teammates. Some kids were disgusted by J-town and wanted nothing to do with them. Intramural championships would thus easily amass every season there on out.

Senior Year

Substance filled summer campouts would continue into the final year. The second Mike's tent popped up the sessions followed wherever they camped out. This year, however, would be far different from the previous two. Something mysterious would develop.

Excitement to be reunited with his college friends for an entire year would fill Tom's mind every hot summer day in Connecticut.

Partying, unpacking, and organizing rooms for the upcoming semester would immediately take precedent

the moment the three reached the new residence hall-
the townhouses.

It was a cramped drive to college in his old red
truck. Tom's anticipation denied any thought of
frustration for lack of elbowroom. He needed all this
extra furniture for the enlarged living quarters. When
Tom arrived back, he had to drive around the
townhouse parking lot for five minutes in hopes of
finding a close spot. Nevertheless, he parked a
considerable distance from his future temporary home.

He chose not to unload anything once he parked. A
direct shot to the Townhouse's brought a fast pace.
Tom's first moments were not to be filled with labor. He
knew his buds were already partying hard for a couple
days. Guilt had been sitting in Tom for the prior two
days. A couple nights of thorough partying was missed.
The closer he got the quicker his trot. It became obvious
which townhouse was his. He began to chuckle. Outside
his new residence, there were his two roommates
sitting in fold-up cloth chairs, with a red Dixie cup

resting within the arm holder. Mike and Fitzy had liquid support while waiting for the missing piece the entire morning.

A few hugs and laughs brought the spirit up. Unification secured their hopes for another year together. A quick tour was suggested by Fitz, which Tom could not deny. "A stove, a microwave, a big TV, our own rooms," would be bellowed out separately by the three. The ritual, which had been performed since sophomore year, then immediately took place in Tom's empty upstairs bedroom. They all took their stashes out.

In accordance with tradition, the buds would journey up into the clouds and then immediately head outside. A great new attribute about their new residence hall, aside from the three living together, was the beautiful green. The grass was perfectly maintained. This they planned would be the location they were to play Frisbee every beautiful day on, rather than Inty's green on the otherside of campus. Above all, throwing the Frisbee stoned with his friends brought Tom the greatest joy.

However, with the ritual being conducted, there she was again, the only girl that magnetized Tom, bringing in a cardboard box into a townhouse. "She lives here too!" Tom thought.

Tom couldn't leave alone an attraction he had never felt before toward a female student. The obsession was stronger than his urge to get high. In years past Tom made connections, but he never felt this power before. He couldn't avoid but feel helpless. To relinquish her image was impossible. Glances were made toward her townhouse every chance he had, while he unloaded all of his paraphernalia into his suite.

A bit taken aback from this situation, he did not show much interest in christening his new organized room with the usual ritual on day two. He told Fitzy as he was interior designing, "I think I am in love!"

A girl he saw around campus throughout the previous three years had now lit a fire within Tom.

Love, in Tom's prior estimation, would come magically through the divine infinite higher power. But in this case he felt he had to act. He just didn't know how. Losing his crush to another man ran through the twenty-one year olds mind constantly.

The time came when Tom and Whitney were both outside the townhouses. Fitzy, being the great friend he was would set Tom up as they were having a toss. The shy young man was put into a situation he could not have created on his own.

With his butt on the grass following a dive and, with a feeling of both humiliation and comfort, Tom was now to embark on the journey adoration had provided. It was both Tom and Whitney Stanton's senior year in college.

The day Whitney entered Tom's life, senior year, was one day prior to the opening day of fall courses. It was a big year for the three friends who were no longer living in the dorms. The senior townhouses would now be considered home for two semesters. It was a great set-up. The three purposefully picked the townhouse that housed three, while others housed as much as six.

The first couple days upon arrival, in late August 2003, were a complete blur. As blackouts were a means to enhance tribal status, the first couple townhouse evenings raised the bar between the three. Tom, Mike, and Fitz had established quite the group of friends by senior year- some were wrestlers, some were partiers, some didn't play Frisbee, and some were computer nerds. A handful of Jerrytown girls hung out in Townhouse Three daily as well.

Acclaim brought the fellow extremists in. The whole lot of them wanted to make unforgettable moments while not remembering it. It was pretty stupid, but they yearned for it. Younger wrestling teammates were stuck on to Tom like flies on shit. Humbleness is very attractive, as he led by example, not by words.

The friends, who also wrestled, were the type who also enjoyed all-nighters. Mike too was one of those guys who stayed up on campus with a random group of three until the sun would be seen rising from atop the rail bridge. Tom was in and out of this crowd in prior years.

The conversation following a night without recollection would highlight the moments one could not recollect, yet the others could. Street wrestling in the center of the downtown strip, for instance, was a hot topic for the surrounding drunks on the second night back. Tom woke up that morning and asked Mike why his elbow hurt so badly, in which Mike replied, "You tried to double leg me and I tossed you. Yeah, everyone was laughing."

"I'm going to skip class. Let's just go throw the biz," Tom replied.

The "biz," as Tom called it, would be the tool that united Whitney Stanton and himself outside the townhouses. TH 3 was home for Tom, which was about a hundred yards down from Whit's townhouse, number thirty. The townhouses only housed seniors. Thus, with the majority of residents holding the legal age, alcohol was rushing through the pipes everyday, no matter which townhouse. There wasn't one dry townhouse. Neighboring the turf football field/intramural field also made the townhouses quite inviting on game days.

Springfield College was a tiny college, but they did party hard by all means. Number three had the fewest parties, but when they did it was huge and legendary. It seemed everyone on campus came to their parties, which ultimately filtered onto the green.

Every townhouse was designed in the same manner- casual living quarters and kitchen downstairs, with bedrooms upstairs. The exterior of the buildings held a square block shape, as the exterior walls were made completely out of brick. The first floor had exterior windows in the front and back. Around back, the kitchen was illuminated all day by the southern sun.

Being the furthest room from the entrance, the kitchen served as the back exit as well, which walked out into a small fenced in green, overlooking the turf field. The name of the turf field was "The Pride's Den," in accordance with the school's nickname- Springfield Pride. Views from the top balcony, which every townhouse had, provided the best angle to watch a football, Frisbee, or lacrosse game.

The central location of the town houses made practice, games, or goofing around, for Jerrytown very convenient. Every member could see when the biz was flying. Thus, there was a large crowd of Frisbee throwers out nearly every day senior year, but this year they could blast The Dead, Stringcheese, or Phish from the speakers put on the kitchen windowsill. The townhouses also brought tailgating to another realm, as residents could get smashed in their own home while watching the game live with no repercussions.

Furthermore, down time was even fun. The seventy inch TV in the front living room provided easy entertainment after a session, especially when Fitzy had 'The Truth News' on. Upstairs though was much different. The bedrooms each only had a tiny window for insignificant natural light, with the exception of the second floor balcony's glass door off of Tom's room. The atypical three a.m. occurrences would happen in these small rooms.

In consideration of attending a relatively small school, along with befriending Fitzy, a social butterfly, Tom too seemed to know everyone. He said hi to everyone on campus. Nonetheless, it was the bars that held the best means of social interaction with all the walks of life. Everyone went out. Tom and Mike were the exception to the majority however. They would go out maybe once a week years prior, if that. Fitzy, on the other hand, was out every Thursday thru Sunday, even though he never really had any money- coming from a single parent income. He always still found ways to get free drinks. The great thing senior year brought was the ability to use their true identification.

Those conversations that man would have! Fitzy would lock himself into conversations with random people each and every night out. Subliminally, Fitzy targeted unsuspecting peers who seemed kind enough to buy the big guy a couple cocktails. Conversely, the occasional nights Tom went out would be spent in silence until Fitzy introduced the attractive young man to his new bar friends. If Tom heard something he could relate to he would intervene. Conversations were made with males or females, black or white, Fitzy didn't discriminate. What he loved most of all was the girls who sponsored his night out by buying him drinks.

At the bars, just as in the dorms, Fitzy and Mike would go at it. Mike knew Fitzy best and could push his buttons like no other. The big guy loved to argue politics. It was actually quite theatrical at the bars, as Mike purposefully antagonized Fitz to get a reaction in front of the group of the people buying drinks. The crowd was never disappointed.

One night out Fitzy justified his stance, "Sure you can call me an extreme conservative. I favor small government, war if necessary, no welfare, no immigrants, no universal healthcare, and guns. What's wrong with that?"

The townhouse hosted the same substance. Confrontations again senior year ran awry, especially with the "conservative" news channel being on twenty-four-seven, just as it was in Tom and Mike's dorm room - "The Truth News." Mike, again held nothing back in their temporary home after a couple drinks. "The Truth News' is actually the furthest thing from the truth. Dumbass."

He would remind Fitz that the entire daily broadcast was fictional theatre. The ideology presented was merely fear mongering and propaganda, which was performed to plant the seed of anger and dissent in the mind. Mike said, "Believing editorials and opinions will not provide what truly exists. You are simply receiving the nature of the animal."

Nonetheless, "The Truth" logo would appear on the screen five separate times throughout the commercial breaks during any thirty minute newscast. The logo would be surrounded by symbolic words such as freedom, patriotism, or united we stand. But to Mike, it was a fraud. The true American citizen that paid all their taxes was never represented. Tom felt the same, but did not disclose his lack of empathy towards the news channel.

The arguments actually occurred more often in the townhouses as the three were now under the same roof constantly. Disgust was made clear to Fitz about all politicians, not just right-wingers, wherein Mike made clear that both Fitzy's party, as well as the liberals, made fools of the Americans.

Mike could not hide the fact that he greatly cared for the future. It was clear he was aroused by the cause and effect of synthetic chemicals upon nature, and our wasteful nature toward nonrenewable resources. Most of all he wanted to share all his disturbing research on irresponsible politicians with Fitzy; all in order to win the argument.

One late night in the living room, Mike meandered on about an awesome fall course he took up- Nonrenewable resources. "In our nonrenewable resource class we have read about this folk legend M. King Hubbert. Ever heard of him Fitzy?"

"Na."

"He knew a time would come when world oil production would no longer increase. Supply would no longer meet the demand. Hubbert, an American Geologists, published early predictions back in 1969 displaying the facts. At that time he formed a graph through intense mathematical analysis that displayed a bell shaped curve. The graph predicted that the world would reach its peak oil production in 2000. This theory we call "Hubbert's Peak". Yeah, maybe he was a crazy scientist, but his prediction of when U.S. oil production would reach its peak came true."

"Oil is unlimited Mike," Fitz said.

"If you say so," Mike replied, "See Fitz, society's stability has been provided by cheap oil, no doubt, but lets just say hypothetically, in the absence of that providential commodity, what will become of such a complex system built dependent on the very vehicle for our rapid technological and structural evolution."

"Bull shit Mike," Fitz responded, "There is so much shale available in Canada."

"Ha, not when it uses more fuel to extract it than is produced. How could our most educated society dissipate such a valuable tool?"

"Just watch, in accordance with the universe," Mike said, "Nature holds the power to balance itself and repair our destruction. However, if the self-interested man continues to hold the assumption that he is greater than nature and has every right to manipulate and control it, WE ARE DOOMED! Why can't we call history the truth?"

Mike made it clear to Fitzy that oil was diminishing rapidly pre-2001. He knew a brief solution for an incurable pending crisis was found in Iraq. It would serve as the ideal landscape to procure a bounty of oil. "We just needed an illusion to justify invasion and occupation." But to Mike, he wasn't only bothered by the false pretense presented for war. The lack of knowledge shared to the American public on the pending oil crisis was as egregious. "Ten years ago we should have invested fortunes into alternative energy!"

World peak oil was never discussed on "The Truth News" either. Nevertheless, for every other manipulated topic discussed on each newscast Fitzy would hold a similar view. Everything! Not once in their four years together had Fitzy considered a different perspective.

The war was discussed by far the most in the townhouses-"Operation Freedom". Fitzy considered the counter attack in Iraq, in response to the terrorist attacks, the most important precedence this country would ever put forth. He told Tom during one of his usual speeches, accompanied by a thirty pack, "We should just nuke them. They won't bother us then. Bomb them all. We're fighting people that hate us! It is a rapidly changing world and we must control this!"

Mike responded. "Do you know why they hate us so much?"

"Fitzy, one thing we never consider in this country are the United Nation's sanctions placed on foreign nations. By 2001, when President Bush was sworn into office, the Iraqi people had suffered eleven years of dire sanctions applied. These sanctions blocked food importation, medicine, and also necessary manufacturing equipment. This policy of elimination was forced on by demands of the United States and England. 'The United Nations seized all of Iraq's oil wealth, paying six figure salaries to bureaucrats in New York and Geneva'ᵛ. By the end of sanctions, in 2003, 1.7 million Iraqis had died from starvation and lack of medicine, counting only children under the age of 5 and adults over the age of 60. Under the guise of demanding Iraq's disarmament, the United Nations had succeeded in killing more Iraqi people with its sanctions policy than all the nuclear, chemical and biological weapons of mass destruction ever used in history. Disturbingly, 'the United Nations had already destroyed every weapon system in the country before its inspection teams pulled out of Iraq in 1998'[vi]. Iraqi people didn't want war. Furthermore, how were the Iraqi's supposed to have productive talks with a power who forced so many hardships. Nevertheless, in back room talks with American Intelligence Assets following 9/11, Iraqi diplomats made clear they would cooperate fully with the United States, as they held hopes to end the miserable sanctions."

"Sadly, our need to impose dire circumstances upon people of an unfavorable dictator has wasted our 'financial resources and the talent of future generations'[vii]. So we knew there were no weapons of mass destruction in Iraq, but we still went to war for it. There is substantial evidence that many efforts were made by American Intelligence Assets to notify the government of Iraq's cooperation. The attacks of 9/11 were also disclosed prior to the deadly September day. So Fitzy, what if we spy on someone, get imperative national security information, and then either do nothing about it or flip the truth. I'd say the system of government espionage is ass backwards. I just don't get how you can favor this clearly immoral war. Why are men who knew information that could have saved thousands of lives, but suppressed this truth, not guilty of one crime?"

"It's clear as day Fitz! Our voice has been removed by a group of men who are driven by the philosophy-something for nothing. 'Our leaders promote get rich quick schemes for their Beltway Bandit friends in the oil and defense establishments'[viii]. On March 19, 2003, the night we bombed Iraq, America would no longer be the world's moral leader."

On this occasion Tom became quite cross. It was a rare moment in their friendship that Tom couldn't hold his opinion in. "Fitz, there are good men there, just as there are bad men here. You can't invade a country you fabricate the facts about- harboring terrorists and weapons of mass destruction. Are you going to call me a terrorist because I think the war is wrong? What's wrong with you, you have no problem killing so many innocent peaceful people!"

"Damn right! They're interrupting our freedoms. They're altering our way of life. You got to show what you're capable of sometimes. It's psychological." Fitzy smiled.

To Fitzy the conversation was considered good fun, but as Tom told Fitzy, "I have no say in what happens. We aren't supposed to avoid this war."

Mike no doubt backed Tom. Mike said, "The facts speak for themselves. Lets check the computer." Consequently, all the facts available on the computer checked by Mike made Tom's stance appear true. Many innocent people had died in the war since 9/11 and to Tom it seemed as if the tool of brainwashing had worked within Fitzy. To Tom, his society paid little attention to the trenches of battle, and rather, put all their belief in newscasters and politicians who were paid to form a negative interpretation.

In these terms, Tom always kept a phrase from his high school tech ed teacher in mind, which was more philosophical than technical, "All the prospects life provides is clearly developed through the law of attraction. Very simple Tom!"

Yes, Tom was quiet, yet overtly friendly, always smiling while passing someone on the sidewalk, or quickly glancing for eye contact in the halls to acknowledge a peer. Tom attracted many. Indeed, he was a good-looking kid. He was medium build with no body fat, straight sandy blonde hair that hung just below his eyebrows. Beautiful Carolina blue eyes pierced on first glance. He was a specimen. His muscles were cut-up, though, not overgrown. Muscles for wrestling were trained for stamina, not bulk. Since he stopped lifting to pursue Frisbee and tried out yoga on campus, his body type became more lean.

Senior year was the final season of competitive wrestling. Tom and Mike were named captains of the wrestling team in the preseason meeting. Coach Bly knew all the antics the two had performed, but still felt they were most worthy. Tom was known around campus for many things- the kid that rose from the dead, Frisbee burnout, golf cart thief. But Tom stood out from the crowd and Bly knew this. In the private preseason captain meeting with Mike and Tom, Bly told the two, "Just keep doing what you're doing. Let's get three team championships in a row. Individually, you both should win your weight class and qualify for nationals."

So humble, Tom didn't even realize the attention he received everywhere he went. He didn't mind that random people visited his townhouse every evening. The lifestyle that was brought on when the three roommates partied, in order to witness another historic incident, did not hinder wrestling. Conduct did not improve Tom's skill though.

The less popular majors he chose in plant science and landscape architecture severely faltered academically come senior year. What complicated matters most, was Whitney.

There was little known about Whitney aside from his attraction. Tom's courses had nothing to do with Whitney's graphic design courses. Mike, on the other hand, shared a couple pre-requisite computer courses with her. The two, Tom and Whitney, had never talked before senior year. They somehow avoided talking to each other on the tiny campus, even though they were strongly attracted to each other since freshman year.

The first time Whitney, eighteen at the time, had seen Tom; she thought he was super hot. Junior year, she thought the legend of the fall in Pittsfield was a bit ridiculous and careless, but she dug him nonetheless. Deep down she subliminally didn't like him receiving attention from all the other girls who were after him.

Nevertheless, contact was finally made that August afternoon when all of the seniors were returning to school. Fitzy and Tom were just tossing biz outside on the green with a red Dixie cup. For Tom, following the miraculous diving catch, the most important person would instantly become Whitney. All it took to get the two together was a big throw from Fitzy.

Her appearance was unique for Tom's previous standards. Tom never really had an attraction to short hair on the opposite sex, but it looked so right on Whitney. She had a round face with chubby cheeks and an enormous smile. Her figure was athletic, which stood five-six and weighed near a hundred twenty pounds. She didn't play any sports though.

Tom too was no dedicated athlete, but he was still performing at a very high level. Enjoyment came in hitting the pipe and playing some Frisbee every day, but that was the extent of his daily drug use, aside from a mushroom trip every now and then. Whitney was the same way in that sense. She enjoyed creating a good vibe with the help of a minimally harmless foreign substance.

The three roommates were so close and knew each other so well that when Fitzy noticed Tom looking over at a girl watching the two Jerrytown members tossing biz about seventy-five yards away, he gave Tom the point- extending his right arm out directing Tom with the Frisbee. The sign to show Tom where to run was the same as Fitz had used during games.

Little did Tom know, the girl he adored had went out and bought a Frisbee earlier that day with the intention of stirring up a conversation with the boys. Whitney had been watching Tom the first couple days they had been back. Fantasies ran rampant of a future together. Tom, conversely, would never have ventured over and talked to her himself. Fitzy had quite the radar for the opposite sex and would attack a target in a moment's notice, even though he rarely got lucky. If he did, it was always with a large drunk lady. This time he sent in the stud first.

"Go, start running, I'll set you up," Fitz yelled as he pointed.

"Fitzy don't embarrass me!"

Fitzy put every pound of his weight into this throw. He could easily throw a Frisbee a hundred yards. This overhand hurl was no exception. Tom was pretty fast, but not overwhelming. He had the strange ability though to track a Frisbee to the exact location it was going to fall.

With a full sprint in motion, Fitzy let the biz fly in the direction of the girl. Embarrassment began to fill Tom's mind. Still, he sprinted as fast as he could after it. Fitzy threw it exactly at the girl. He sure humiliated Tom.

A dive was necessary... but he did catch it.

Hence, Whitney immediately ran the short distance over to see if the sprawled out twenty-one year old was ok. Heavy breaths were apparent, but he held onto the Frisbee.

"Are you OK?"

"I'm fine. Don't' worry about me."

After speaking, Tom flipped over, and looked up into her brown eyes. He felt an instant charge while he sat on the grass.

"Nice catch."

She smiled and he felt it. A silent magnetic eye contact held for five seconds, in which a yearning for her companionship was planted.

"Yeah, my friend Fitzy can sure launch it." Tom looked over and gave Fitzy a little grin. "My name is Tom and I live in three. What's your name?"

"Oh I know who you are. I'm Whitney Stanton." He became surprised with her response. "You're Thomas Adams, you're a good wrestler."

"You know who I am?" Tom said, "To tell you the truth, I've known who you are since freshman camp."

"My roommates Liz and Diane had a history class with you sophomore year. I kind of know Mike too. I shared a computer class with him."

"Oh, I know them. Are you happy to be back at school with them?" Tom asked.

"Now I am." She smiled before the awkward silence.

"Do you guys want to stop by three later, my roommates are good company?"

"I will, and I will ask my roommates. What time?"

"We have nothing going on, come over whenever."

With the entire discussion taking place while Tom remained on the grass, he finally stood up. "I'll see you later."

Tom's roommate walked quickly towards him the moment Whit turned her back to Tom.

"What's the deal?" Fitzy asked.

"I'm gonna marry her," Tom said.

"She's cute. She have any friends?"

"A couple of her roommates are decent. I had them in a history class a couple years ago. My girl is named

Whitney and she's going to stop bye later. She may bring her friends."

Fitzy grew a huge grin. "I hope so. This year is going to be the best year ever."

Back at TH3, Mike did not seem to have the same sediment as Fitzy. When the two returned and told Mike what transpired in TH3, he replied, "She's gonna take you from us!"

"Shut up. This is our year," Fitzy said.

"Just watch," Mike quickly replied.

A Relationship

Around seven the three girls walked into Three. Mike, Fitzy, another wrestling teammate Scott Uffleman (Uff), and Tom were all just starting to get a buzz from the pong table, which also served as the dining room table. The crew all knew girls were coming over. Hence, they all showered and dressed casually conservative. Tom actually tucked into his jeans the beige J Crew polo shirt he borrowed from Mike. It was a much different presentation than just getting drunk amongst themselves on a week night. Tom spent a couple hours wiping everything down with Mike's vinegar solution. Mike was the only one that didn't change his usual wardrobe, which consisted of a salvation army tee and cargos.

The girls walked in. Whitney looked amazing. She had jeans and a half sweater on with her belly button ring exposed. She could have worn anything and Tom would have held the same position. She held a natural beauty that did not require make-up, but this night she put a little on with her friends help. The other girls dolled themselves up. Fitzy immediately stopped the game of beer pong as they entered, proceeded to put on a new music playlist with pop songs, and then became the great host he always was. Introductions thus transpired, which Fitzy administered. It did make everyone feel comfortable.

As the night moved fast, the group did not go out to get drinks. Fitzy threw the idea out there, but everyone really enjoyed crowding around the beer pong table. There were no more than ten people in the townhouse at one time, still continual conversations and laughter flowed through the night. The group huddle let everyone get to know each other very well.

Tom and Whit played on the same beer pong team, but they did not win any of the three games they would play together. Fitzy, naturally, made sure everyone knew his stance on all world affairs. Whitney's friends weren't that impressed with Fitzy, while Tom and Whit stayed side by side the entire night. Tom discovered Whitney's parents owned a huge condominium community in Florida.

At one it seemed as if everyone was getting tired. Fitzy was laying on the sofa eating chips, he gave up on trying to score when he sensed the girls back away whenever he tried to get closer. Mike was on a stool around the table with his laptop on his lap. Mike was a good looking kid, but it took a lot for a female to excite him. Tom, Whit, and her friends were the only ones remaining sociable around the pong table.

Whitney's roommates told her they were going to walk back to the townhouse, in which Tom quickly responded that he would walk her home, "if it was ok". "Of course," she responded.

It was a quick walk. Tom's mind was filled with so many expectations. Nonetheless, when they reached her townhouse she simply leaned over and kissed Tom's cheek, "I'll see you tomorrow maybe."

Things would continue to develop with every meeting the two shared. The second night they hung out, before a word was said, Tom leaned forward and gave her an Eskimo kiss. The first couple months together felt similar to the first night they shared together- bliss. They talked, drank, and smoked with all of their friends just about every evening. It seemed the more they shared of each other's lives the more they wanted to know. Consequently, the more and more Tom partied though. At the time it was great fun and a matter of no concern, as opening up was quite easy half in the bag.

Tom justified to himself that his need to be intoxicated or high was because it calmed his nerves, especially around Whitney. It did work. He didn't want to mess anything up. There was no doubt he was in love immediately and felt at peace in her presence. All he yearned for was to lay beside her in her single bed and talk the night away.

Come the end of October, it was time for wrestling. Mike and Tom, as captains, held as laid back an approach as any leader could have had. They were stoned every practice and never once forced a confrontation upon a teammate. Ithaca came up real quick. The team wrestled real good, finishing second, while Mike again placed fourth. Tom, on the other hand, who never placed in the prior three opening tournaments somehow made the finals. In the semifinal match again the nationally ranked College of New Jersey opponent Tom somehow hit the sickest ankle roll he ever has performed. Something finally went right against a very difficult opponent.

He did not win the finals match, but he only lost 3-2. Bringing home a second place finish brought Tom into the national rankings- seventh in the country. He could not believe it. It was a big joke to everyone in townhouse three. All the prior college experience he had received by just showing up was demonstrated this final season of his wrestling career. Mike didn't hold any envy, wrestling had been put on the back burner since freshman year.

Being nationally ranked didn't change anything, he just wanted to hang out with Whit.

The winter season daily routine was simple for Tom- go to a few classes, practice, or hang out in Whitney's room the duration of the day.

Tom only lost once the entire season- a 39-1 record. He was doing something right, maybe he was wrestling so hard to impress his lady. She came to all the home meets to cheer on her man.

By the time of the New England Tournament Tom was ranked one. Mike was ranked fourth. It was an easy path to the finals for Tom. Mike, on the other hand, had a disappointing performance for Coach Bly and finished sixth. Mike didn't care, he wrestled hard, but just didn't catch any breaks. A half hour before the finals, Tom asked Mike, "You thinking what I'm thinking?"

"Oh yeah, sess." Mike smiled.

"Oh yes, but where?" Tom asked.

"In the woods, I already smoked there once. I got one bowl pack left. You in champ?" Mike asked.

"Let's do it!"

And so, there was Mike and Tom passing a pipe behind some spruces outside the Roger Williams Athletic Complex.

Back inside the tournament floating, Tom began warming up. He did his usual ten fifty yard sprints five minutes before his match, while the weight class below began its match. He was ready- yes stoned, but he was going to give it his all. Sure enough, he won 4-2 against his Trinity rival. He capitalized again on the lone mistake, not making one himself- The New England College Conference Champ.

Boy did they celebrate in TH3. Whitney sat on the back burner this evening. Everyone else made sure Tom blacked out, ultimately crashing prematurely on the couch for the night. At the point Whit showed up Tom was passed out.

A week later though would be the NCAA Division III National Wrestling Tournament in Dubuque, Iowa. In preparation, Tom had a carefree week of practice. The qualifier was to fly out on Thursday only with the coaching staff. There were no Springfield friends or fans making the trip to Iowa in March.

The brackets were tough out there. Everyone was an All-American caliber wrestler. Placing top eight, to earn All-American accolades, simply came down to who was having the best day. Thursday evening, the night before Nationals began, the Dubuque Convention Center was open for all wrestlers to come on the mats for weight control and to get a sweat going. Tom simply sprinted around the exterior of the eight mats in awe of all the talent. He didn't feel as if he belonged.

Friday, day one of the tournament was most important. Win two matches and you're an All-American. Lose two and you ain't nothing. Tom's first match was against an opponent from Simpson College, a two time All-American. Boy it was a stalemate of a battle. There was not one take down. But Tom kept pushing and pushing. The referee warned the Simpson wrestler for stalling once- not working for a takedown. He was a defensive wrestler, Tom was offensive. In the third and final period, the ref again hit the Simpson wrestler with a stalling penalty, while Tom kept pusching, which resulted in a point for Tom.

UUUUUUUUUNNNNNNNNN. The buzzer sounded, Tom won his first match at nationals. One more victory meant he was an All-American. A framed All-American certificate with his name would go on the Springfield College wall of fame if he won one more. His second match, however, was against the number two seed in the nation. He was a former national champ. The opponent from the University of Iowa- Stevens point seemed ginormous compared to Tom. In the opening handshake he nearly crushed Tom's hand.

Nevertheless, Tom attacked. He actually got the first take down on an amazing single leg. But Tom's mat skills, bottom position especially, were subpar. He couldn't hold the opponent down. It was 2-1 after the first period. Second period started with a bang. Tom again went after the same single leg takedown from the neutral position he chose to start the second period. Again, Tom grabbed the leg and brought it up between his legs, this time, however, the University of Iowa wrestler fought it by sprawling his hips away. A struggle led the two toward the out of bounds circle with full momentum. The strong opponent through in an overhook and an underhook. He then used Tom's force against himself. Tom's legs ended up pointed at the ceiling, but his head ended up crashing into the scorer's table.

The entire arena gasped. Tom was out for a minute. When he came to, he simply said, "I gotta finish this coach."

The trainer nodded to Bly. Tom would nod to coach, "I can suck this up, I think?" He walked back out and put his foot on the green line to begin. But it wasn't Tom back on the mat, he was done. He was in fog no drug could provide. Tom made it through the match, but he got rode like a pony at the state fair. He lost 8-3.

Tom was defeated. He knew he couldn't perform to the best of his ability, but he told Bly he was going to finish what he started with tears in his eyes. The third match was against a tough Augsburg kid who was not happy to be in the losers bracket. If Tom won he would still be an All-American.

But he was no All-American. Nothing felt right. He was embarrassed 10-1. There it was, wrestling was over. Subsequent to the humiliating defeat Tom put on his wrestling hoody ran to darkest deepest corner of the convention center and balled for hours.

Coach Bly finally found him when the All-American round had concluded for the day. "Let's go get drunk on me bud!" Bly said

Tom finally cracked a smile. Through a couple drinks Tom was back to normal. He called Whit and told her everything that transpired. "I can't wait to see you," were her final words to close the conversation.

By the end of senior year Tom had no time for his best friends, he was barely able to make time for Jerrytown intramural games, even though Whit did immensely enjoy tossing the biz on the green with the J-town crew. She didn't play on J-town however, because of night courses.

During the spring, consequently, the only time he saw Mike and Fitz was at J-town practice or in their townhouse before he would leave to hangout with Whitney for the night. He never went out to the bars anymore. Now he was becoming a closet drunk. A flask of whiskey always accompanied Tom to her townhouse. He wouldn't even tell her about it or share it with her.

Henceforth, by the time of graduation, which Tom barely reached, the inseparable ones wanted to advance their relationship. Positively correct Mike, and Fitzy were not involved in the plan. Only Whitney held a job as a waitress, but they still thought it possible to afford their own place.

Hartford

Subsequent to graduation, Mike and Fitzy chose to remain in school for Master degrees in their targeted fields. Tom just wanted to start a life with Whitney. He barely held on to receive his bachelors in plant science and landscape design.

Tom's mother brought to his attention one night before graduation that the first floor was vacant in Hartford, as Miss Foley had passed away. Wendy loved Whitney and wanted to provide as much assistance as the two would need. Whit's care after Tom meant for his survival and mother knew that by this point. Thus, the two decided they were going to move into the two family house Tom's family owned, where Tom had grown up in Hartford. Wendy had taken up responsibility of the house after Robert died and she moved to Wethersfield. It was still in her son's name. In a responsible manner, Wendy banked all the rent money she received in order to maintain the property. The rest of the money was stored for Tom's college loans. A free house was quite a graduation present.

Living together was one thing, but marriage was of no interest to Tom. His parents' did not last, why would his. Nevertheless, he loved Whitney like no other, even though they came from far different lives.

Whit grew up in Kissimmee, Florida, also as an only child. She obviously was her bid daddy's baby. And her father, Willy Stanton, still treated her as his baby into adulthood. Well off, her dad provided her with a college bank account that he would add an allowance to every month.

She, however, did not touch his money. The money all went into savings. She earned all her college spending money as a waitress throughout. Willy, a very wealthy man, yearned to make the final decision with everything in her life. The Stanton's owned a large group of condos called the Sunny Side Condos, which were in the beginning process of doubling in size when Whit and Tom first met. Willy bought four hundred acres of neighboring land, which was going to house more of his condos in Kissimmee. It was to have a forked entranceway, ultimately, connecting both properties. Magnificent landscaping shaped the land's maximum potential.

Sunny Side made most of their money through timeshares. The upscale condos ranged from small two-bedroom units to spacious four-bedroom dwellings. People would stay for golf vacations or Disney trips, as the condos were in a central location. The landscape was immaculate. It was comparable to that of a golf course. Plant beds were rotated with fresh mulch every other month. Trees, annuals, perennials, and shrubs would be planted and pruned according to the season.

Willy felt if the grounds were pleasing than the people would feel at peace and want to live and stay there. Everyone wanted to be a part of something, especially if it was flawlessly reputable. Willy shared his success with his best friend growing up named Jim Arnold. The two knew each other since the days at Kissimmee Elementary School. Uncle Jim, as Whitney knew him, was in charge of the grounds, condo maintenance, and landscape architecture.

Uncle Jim too had a crew of four Guatemalans' under his supervision, in which most of them had worked for Willy for over twenty years. The Guatemalan crew lived for free in a condo for the ten months they worked on the property; they then returned home to their families for two months. They were very efficient. The four were of small stature but they could work, never stopping for a second without Jim's consent.

Through long days in the sun they never grumbled once about labor or being away from their family. Jim treated them pretty well. His token of appreciation was shared through an invitation to join Willy and himself for a couple beers during break or after work in the grounds garage.

The Guatemalan's loved Whitney. They had watched her grow up and always showed her joy. Uncle Jim, moreover, always thought of Whitney as the little girl he watched grow. But with her college degree he was a bit worried. He always thought he was the next in line behind big Willy. And Willy had some lung condition that was worsening. Whitney called the same man an uncle, who considered sabotaging Whitney's chance at inheriting the condos. Through all the labor he invested over thirty years, Jim lived for free the entire time. Home was a luxurious 2-bedroom condo receiving free cable, electrical, medical, etc. He also received a six figure annual salary. All the employees (grounds, custodial, maintenance) lived for free during their employment. Jim, however, amassed no savings, as he loved to drink, eat, and pay strippers.

Big Willy did share his wealth generously. In one shot, the Stanton's were able to pay all of Whitney's tuition off when payment was due after each semester. She chose graphic design so she could have purpose to join the family business. In college, she brainstormed many ideas- marketing, advertising, and publicity. Daniel Stanton, Whit's mom, took care of all the bookwork, which Whit hoped to take over one day.

In Hartford, sadly, Tom started drinking to excess every day. In college he seemed normal with his binges, yet after everyone else stopped blacking out he continued.

A free place to live was a fortunate situation for Tom after graduation, even though he was drinking heavily and held no job. Nevertheless, the two moved into the vacant first floor apartment in the house Tom inherited from his father. Tom's forty year old cousin

Mark lived upstairs, who handed the rent checks over to Wendy. Wendy Adams continued to live in Wethersfield, two minutes away from Tom's two family house in Hartford.

A substantial police salary allowed her to move out of the two family house, even though she considered it home for so long. But she wanted to leave that place. It would always be her husband's house. The house would remain in the family's hands with Tom away at school, as it was placed in Tom's name before Robert Adams' death.

When Tom and his mom moved out of the city, his cousin moved in, above Ms. Foley. Mark was a painter. He was a good guy that got a good deal renting from his family. Ten years older than Tom, by the time Tom finished college, Mark was already married with children.

He never really did pay Tom much attention though. The most time the two spent together was when Mark helped Tom move in. He knew very well that Tom was a closet drunk. Tom snuck away every thirty minutes, Mark didn't want to deal with a drunk in that house again. He had a few nasty runs-ins with intoxicated Robert. Once settled, the only time Tom would come up to visit Mark and his kids was when the booze ran out. Mark didn't criticize. He didn't want to make waves.

To Whitney, things appeared to be going well at first on the first floor. She had become familiar with New England weather from attending college in Massachusetts and enjoyed it. A job was quickly found waitressing at Chiles. Living alone together was far different from sharing a single mattress with Tom and a townhouse with three others. Whit couldn't read the signs, as Tom, at this point, was heading toward the downward spiral his father had fallen through. He was going out all night more and more with all his old high school buds.

Again, he put himself in a situation where reaching the blackout condition gained praise. Whitney didn't think much of his conduct when he would return home late. However, she found a distraction in interior designing their apartment.

Visits were made to all the local flea markets to discover distinct ornaments and knickknacks. Whit had purchased an old popcorn maker, old tins, old milk jugs, a flag with thirteen stars. The house began having a nostalgic feel. However, month after month of decorating with unique items, Tom was getting worse. Worry started to set in Whitney's mind after a year of this conduct, along with the knowledge of Robert Adams' fate. It was obvious that Tom was a drunk.

Whitney would always be awake when he would come home from his late night binges. The simple question, "We're have you been Tom?" would always evolve into the same spat.

"Why does it matter? I'm home now," Tom would respond.

"Tom I get lonely."

"I'm young! I can have fun! Why don't you call one of your x's, whore," Tom said. Jealousy and pain could not hide when he was drunk.

"Tom you can't control yourself. You are DRUNK everyday! You can change this, but I can't change my past!"

"Shut up Whit. I'm sleeping on the couch." Tom would conclude with the same antidote every occasion. But when he woke up, he didn't have any recollection of his words or actions.

Meanwhile, the strength of love somehow brought them toward the idea of creating a life. Whitney thought it would make things better.

Whitney became pregnant in 2005. On the outside Tom appeared fearless. At the first mention of pregnancy, unemployed Tom knew what he had to do. There were very few high paying local jobs looking for a landscaper with a plant science degree.

Nevertheless, he sent out his resume to five different landscape firms. Within a week, he accepted a job. Now he would be making minimum wage for the landscape design company *Garden Paths*. Adequate with no rent due.

The transition into forty hours a week was manageable at first. The company in fact loved his expertise. He would recommend certain plantings within symmetrical arrangements around estates, houses, pools, parking lots, etc. Nevertheless, there was little growth that could be made in a little company struggling to survive.

Tom was now beginning the day before work with a shot and a beer, always making sure to stop at the gas station for gum. As he would start in the morning he would conclude into the evening.

Whitney would often call her mother crying during her first trimester. "Tom comes home drunk everyday from work! I don't know what's going to happen."

The two other buds ended up both getting their master's from Springfield College, while Tom was enrolled in the same graduate program as Robert. Mike's was in Environmental Science and Fitzy's was in Political Science. Indeed, as soon as they heard word of the pregnancy they flew down to see Tom's place and celebrate.

They visited Hartford prior, but this visit wasn't like the others when all three blacked out downtown. Only one would this time. Visitors were more of a chore to the host, but Mike and Fitzy were the exception.

The two were shocked that Tom owned a beautiful house in a beautiful section of Hartford. He never mentioned the arrangements much prior. Fitz and Mike were most stoked to see Whitney's belly showing the moment they arrived.

When the three got to talking in Tom's yellow living room, sitting on either the brown pull out sofa or matching love seat, Mike and Fitzy disclosed their future plans. They had to impress Tom, as he had made the first bright impression. Mike was moving to California to work on water and air pollution with a firm in California. Fitzy actually had received an associate professor position in house and was going to receive a free doctorate. Tom didn't have to explain his future. To him, plans seemed to be clearly laid out.

This night was going to be a last hurrah, even though no one mentioned it. The two were excited to go out and again see Tom's hometown. The difference now was that the guests calmed down a lot. They were not the same Townhouse Three roommates. Mike quit smoking and barely drank. Fitzy drank a six pack a week. Tom, on the other hand, drank a liter of whiskey a day chased down by a number of beers, as well as, smoked an eighth a week.

Reminiscent discussions stirred with Whit in the living room for two hours until Tom started itching for the fire water. "Let's get this party started," was abruptly thrown out there.

"Let's do it!" Fitzy said.

The decision was made on where to go, the choice of where to visit was the bar Tom frequented most- "The Pit".

'The Pit' was sure kicking that Friday night. The beers and whiskey were running through the boys' blood with a fierce speed. Mike had only a few though. Tom would run out to the car every thirty minutes to spark up. Tom and Fitz would rotate in buying the round. Fitzy went on, while Mike chimed in, about his student debt. Mike said, "It's one of the only things you can't file bankruptcy for. What a joke! It's not education, it's big business"

By the forth round of whiskey shots accompanying five beers, Fitzy looked at Tom and called it quits. Tom was another story; he was just then getting his shine on. The bar as a pedestal the entire night was Tom's plan. Mikc and Fitz wanted to explore other bars and meet some women. Tom didn't want to proceed with that idea, he was velcroed to the stool. When confronted about a time to leave, Tom simply replied, "Boys I'm just getting started. What happened to Townhouse Three for life?"

Mike responded, "Dude all of us, you included, got much bigger things going on than to get shitfaced. One of us has to drive home. Look at you man. You're going to have a kid. What a fucking mess!"

Tom smiled and waved the bartender down, "One more round, make mine a double."

The other two looked at each other warily, didn't say a word, and took the shot upon its arrival. "Let's get home and hang like we used to," Tom said. He read between the lines, but did not try to restore Mike and Fitz's confidence for his future.

The ride home was difficult for Tom. The two responsible twenty-three year olds told Tom how it was. Mike began, "Tom, honestly, I'm worried for you. You're a mess. You look like shit..."

"Yeah, overtired." Fitzy interrupted.

"You're going to be a dad man. How are you going to manage? You don't make much money and what's

Whitney going to do- waitressing, stay at home? Do you know how much day care is?" Mike shook his head while he drove Tom's extended cab black Chevy truck.

"I know I gotta tighten things up, but this is supposed to be fun. Like old times!" Tom had no more to say.

"Tom, nothing stays constant in this universe, things are in both habitual and irregular motion, and change is the result. If I were the same as sophomore year I would be concerned," Mike replied and continued on.

"All I know is that when my ashes spread out on this land, I want to contribute my healthy nature to strengthen our great mother!"

The remainder of the ride was quiet. Upon arrival, the three slowly entered the house as bedtime approached. Whitney pulled out the sofa prior, in order to place out extra linen and pillows. She couldn't stay up to this hour though. Tom went into his bedroom closet, grabbed the bubbler, but the two assumed sleeping on the sofa's. "You guys going to bed. I thought we'd rip it then eat some nachos, just like the old days Fitzy. You remember how we rolled, right?"

Mike seemed as though he had already passed out on the love seat. Fitzy got up from lying on the sofa. Stood face to face with Tom. "You can't do this shit anymore. Grow up."

Fitz tossed the pillows to the head position. Bed would be provided by the bed-sofa. He kicked off his shoes, spread the blanket, and hopped to bed. Tom turned off the lights for the boys, all to find the porch for himself. In the morning the three shared a quick melancholy Sunday breakfast. Then the two left. Mike left Tom with a couple words, "Take care of that girl and kid."

The three would instantaneously lose touch the moment Fitz and Mike left Hartford. The once monthly phone calls would disappear too.

On the surface the future looked great for Tom and Whit. The two young adults had saved up a lot of money. Whit saved all of her and Tom's earnings into one account. They didn't pay for rent or a mortgage. He only spent money on booze. She saved every penny she earned from waitressing into the college bank account her father made for her. Tom's job provided money for life's needs too. They had accumulated around thirty thousand dollars in the few years living together. Talks spawned about building their dream house in Connecticut on a couple acres, when they took into consideration selling Tom's house to Mark. Whitney would design the interior while Tom would design the plantings. However, Whitney's mother Danielle thought it would be best for her to move back home to Florida.

"Whitney, if you're not happy come home."

"Mom I can't leave Tom, but there's nothing I can do to help. He seems so sad. Angry. But Mom, he depends on me! He will get better. He'll get over this."

"He can come too. He may just need to grow up a little bit," Danielle Stanton said, "You're father had to."

"He doesn't want to move in with my parents. We have a lot of money saved up for our own house mom. It would be taking a huge step back."

"Well why don't you put some money into the shack. Dad always wanted to renovate that old place."

"...That actually sounds like a good idea, we'll see what Tom thinks mom. Love you."

Whitney's mom thought it would be best if the couple put their money into remodeling a small farmhouse that was behind the Stanton mansion, which also neighbored the condo's. The shack was the last remaining building on the property still in existence when the land was bought in 1910 by Willy's twenty-two year old grandfather.

Willy didn't want to tear it down. Thus, it remained vacant for years. He stored air filters for the condo's air units throughout the first floor. The only maintenance it received was a new roof and monthly visits by the condo's outsourced exterminator. Willy didn't mind the idea of having someone else put money into his property after he was told of his wife's idea. With the knowledge of Tom's disease, Big Willy planned to weed that boy out.

The idea of moving sounded good to Tom when Whitney addressed it, "My mother said we could live in the shack behind her house for free. She said we could fix it up if we want"

"Hmmm. What's wrong with this place? We have it easy here; my cousin and his kids don't bother us. They hand us money for rent every month. It's the best set-up ever!"

"I know Tom, but … I don't think this is where I want to raise my child. I don't think it's good you're around your old friends. And we could actually collect from two tenants if we move."

"Oh… true, well I can give your place a shot. We'll be able to save money still. I'm just gonna have to find a new job," Tom said.

"You should have no problem with that. It's landscaping season year round. I'm sure my dad can help you, he knows everybody."

"When are we going to move?" Tom asked.

"Maybe in a few months, why don't you plan a day for your leave of absence."

Sure enough in January, four months before the birth of their son, they moved south to Kissimmee. They drove Tom's truck down along with a packed trailer he bought for the move. Drunk the whole ride down from his spiked Gatorade, he wouldn't object to anything even if it was the worse possible scenario for him.

Sunny Side Condo Community

The moment Tom pulled into the Sunny Side driveway he was in awe. It was the most beautifully designed thirty acres he ever saw. Florida golf courses were in ignominy by the appearance of the condo grounds. The plants all seemed as if the higher power placed them in their individual location to serve some greater than life purpose. Sixty condo's were all reserved when Tom first arrived. The tennis courts, basketball courts, and swimming pools were all occupied with joyous behavior. The huge construction site, that was to double the size of the Sunny Side Community, neighbored the condos. Excavators, bulldozers, huge concrete drain pipes, all spread out on Willy's new land.

Tom had never made the trip down south, even as he and Whit were together for almost three years. Her mom would come and visit her in college, but Tom never had an interest to make the trip to see where Whitney grew up. And, Whitney lived in a mansion her entire life. As far back as she could remember she had a butler and housekeeper in her house. Help was told to disinfect and sanitize every square foot with the most innovative chemical technology. The help too lived in the neighboring condos.

The two arrived at the Stanton estate on a bright afternoon. Before the homecoming, the two first passed Whitney's mansion on the right, in order to have the gates opened to take the driving tour of Sunny Side. The gated community could only be entered in one way. In passing by Willy's front door, Tom imagined that Big Willy waved to over a hundred people a day. Danielle kept a frozen smirk with each passerby, as she held the knowledge of all the gossip.

Whitney's mom and dad were standing outside the front door when the young couple pulled into the horseshoe driveway overlooking the condo's. There, Willy was standing atop his precise stone steps having an awfully common asthmatic attack. "Here's the pain med's dear," Dr. Wife whispered.

The pavers led Tom to a parking space in front of the house. Ten immense slate steps led to Willy and Danielle, who stood in front of the most expensive stone siding. The landscape was breathtaking around the house. There was not one dead leaf or branch on any of the symmetrical shrubs and trees.

The four shared greetings. Tom and Willy had only met once before in Springfield. The handshake they would share defined the present relationship. Willy's hand wrapped around Tom's, which then squeezed Tom's palm until he cringed. Willy was a clean-shaven large man with quite the double chin. He always wore a Florida Marlins hat and five out of the seven days of the week he wore overalls.

Whitney favored her mother in looks. Danielle Stanton was in very good condition for her age of sixty. She had short hair as well, which was colored strawberry blonde. A smile was always on her face. In the most open manner, she would ask the two to come in and have a seat. As the newcomer walked in he could not help but wince from the pungent aerosol febreze odor. It almost blemished what he was to enter.

Tom could not believe the glow inside the house as he walked into the front lobby. From his viewpoint he could see within six different rooms, as well as up the stairwell. It was the shiniest railing he had ever seen. Every doorway seemed to stretch six feet wide. Each piece of wood had such a fine varnish that the house seemed to illuminate with no lighting. Tom quickly perused the house, while Willy and Danielle went to the kitchen and Whit followed. Tom quickly noticed something very disturbing. The women, conversely, were so excited for the pregnancy.

Following whispers, all three returned to the front hall landing- Willy remained silent. It was apparent with Tom's legs shaking that he was uncomfortable. Tom wasn't afraid of many men with his wrestling background, he thought he could subdue most people. The fear Tom felt inside the mansion didn't exist because Willy Stanton was six foot two and three hundred pounds. Size didn't frighten Tom; it was the contents inside the showcase that first caught his eye the moment he entered the showroom.

Willy's prized collection was locked in a large glass case within the front antechamber. The contents happened to be of all the guns Willy had collected the past forty years. Sixty guns were presented. Of these, a few dated all the way back to the French and Indian

War. There were also more recent semi-automatics standing among the collection.

Willy finally spoke following the brief baby talk walk. The two couples now sat parallel at the dining room table sipping on tea, "So you're having a kid.

"Yes sir."

"Well we got that shack you guys can live in. We can go take a look whenever you want. I love that building for some reason, it has a timeworn look to it." Willy said.

"Sounds good."

They all got up after some small talk and the four walked out the back door toward the shack. "What are you going to do for work out here Tom? I'd offer you something, but Jim says it wouldn't be enough for you to support my daughter," Willy spoke while they walked out the back door.

There was a pause in response. Tom noticed the shack, with the four walking toward it. Quickly Tom would give more attention to selling his story to Willy rather than inspecting the shack. "I've been landscaping for some years now, I have a degree in landscape design and plant science. I should be able to find some work out here. I'm going to start looking for work after we get settled, ya' know. We have about thirty thousand saved up. We'll be fine."

Willy chuckled. "Good luck with that. What do you think of my place?"

"Amazing."

Uncle Jim then drove up in his all terrain vehicle while the four approached the blue shack. Jim got out and walked up to the group. Jim was medium height with a beer gut. His beard had a few grey hairs mixed within the brown. Hair was slightly overgrown, but covered with a lawn fertilizer green hat. He had a wide nose and small eyes.

"Whose this guy?" Jim asked as he pointed and looked Tom up and down- all the knowing who it was.

"Tom Adams," Whitney quickly replied.

Jim looked and smiled at Willy, while sharing a firm handshake with Tom. "What do you do?"

"Landscape," Tom said.

"Oh. Well we don't have any openings here sorry.... See all this land, me and Willy designed it all. We planted most of the stuff twenty-five years ago. Now we sit back and tell people what to do."

Jim's ego quickly grew obvious to Tom.

"My dad built all these condos. We made the land pretty nice huh," Willy added, "People always keep coming back here to stay."

Jim then said, "I've been working here full time with Willy for over forty years now, since I was fifteen. When I started here I was mowing ten acres of turf for Willy Sr. Now after this new construction I'll be overseeing over a hundred acres."

Jim's labor is what brought him family status amongst the Stanton's. He was only considered an Uncle because he dedicated so much of his life to the condos. He was briefly married, but his wife didn't want to be trapped inside a condo. He had been divorced for twenty years when Tom arrived. Whitney told Tom before he met Jim to be prepared, "Uncle Jim gives everyone a hard time." The forewarning didn't impact Tom's opinion.

Before Jim got back on his atv, he chuckled. "Good luck kid, you're going to need it."

The time spent with Jim had abandoned the purpose of their walk briefly. They were now in front of the shack. The vacant home was five hundred feet behind the mansion, in which a long crushed stone driveway led to the shack's front door. The closer Tom got to the house the more it appeared to be old. The blue paint was flaked everywhere. Window shutters were missing, while four windows were shattered.

"Here it is," Willy said.

"Needs some work," Whitney said. She was the first to enter. She gave Tom an uncomfortable smile when eye contact was made inside.

"Sure does, but we have some money," Tom said.

"Do whatever you want... Now, more importantly, what about marriage?" Willy asked.

"Well..."

"Tom, letting you live here for free is what family does. A child with my blood better have a husband and wife as parents. I don't get embarrassed in my own town. I hope you understand."

An awkward silence fell over the four.

"Check out the upstairs bedrooms, they are large," Danielle broke the silence.

Willy then turned away and left. He didn't even bother taking a tour with them.

"He's tough," Danielle said.

"Just ignore him," Whitney said.

"No offense Mrs. Stanton, but Whit knows I think marriage is garbage. Look at my parents."

"I know son."

With that, they continued to study the inside. Each room presented a different issue and problems rapidly accumulated. Crumbling sheet rock, mold, disgusting stained toilets and showers, missing trim, were some of the many issues.

Danielle hugged first Whitney and then Tom after the tour. The concerned mother whispered in Whitney's ear before she headed back to the mansion, "Hang in there."

The second her mother made her departure out the door, Whitney broke down. "I don't want to raise my child in this slum. I'm sorry Tom."

"We can fix it up, we have money. I'll work on it every night... But my concern is that I'm going to put my life savings and hard labor into something that belongs to a man that obviously doesn't respect or trust me."

"Well, what else are we going to do? He just wants us married Tom!" Whitney yelled with her hands over her sodden eyes.

"You were the one that wanted to move out of my house."

"Yeah, so we're here now!" Whitney shouted.

"We'll be fine." Tom hugged Whitney. "I'll find a job. And in the meantime, I'll start getting room by room done."

Whitney smiled.

Tom wasn't fine though. He was overwhelmed with concern. A few months from now he was going to bring a child into this world. He had no job or house. Additionally, he now had to perform labor inside the house he wasn't familiar with in order to give his child good living conditions. Furthermore, alcohol was always present internally. It was the only thing bringing him calm and reassurance that things would be fine. Tom didn't know much carpentry, plumbing, or electrical, but every afternoon he would work on it, subsequent to putting down an empty bottle. He was willing to learn through Youtube searches, as he went.

Later in the day, withstanding Tom's arrival, Willy met with Jim for their daily six-pack break and possible asthmatic episode in the maintenance garage. It was a common occurrence for the two to meet in the garage to shoot the breeze. The breaks sometimes lasted hours. If equipment were down, it would become an all day break- only to take a brief break from the break to look at the broken vehicle for ten minutes. Break, also, was Willy's best chance to hit the pain med stash. Shelves, surrounding the two, were filled with every synthetic herbicide, pesticide, and fertilizer as well. The best equipment available was parked with the e-brakes on. The topic on this day was the "Tom" situation. Willy let the truth be told. "He's a drunk Jim. According to Danielle, he makes Whitney cry everyday. Yeah, he may be a good looking kid, but looks are deceiving."

"And you're going to let him live for free in your place. No labor!" Jim said.

"Yeah, I'm not going to let that fool work here, I hold no doubt he will ruin everything we have created. But what's the worse that can happen if he lives in the shack, that place is worthless. He saved up some money. Let him put it into fixing it up and then she'll kick him out sooner than later. We'll have our baby, plus our first grandkid living behind us. We'll pay for whatever he doesn't do. He may not even make it for the birth."

"Willy, I get a funny feeling, like he's going to try to take this place over right from under our nose."

"Keep a close eye on him Jim." Willy proceeded to take his usual large gulp that consumed half of the beer.

"I'll make his life a living hell boss. Instigate a reaction."

Willy smiled. "Na, let him kick himself in the ass."

The shack wasn't all that bad. It had two floors with two bedrooms upstairs. There was a kitchen, dining room, and living quarters, which encircled the stairwell downstairs. Most importantly, Tom and Whitney enjoyed staying in a house all to themselves. That first day they moved into one of the bedrooms Tom began gutting the other one following a trip for tools at the hardware store. It was to be the baby's. Plastic covered the doorway to block the dust from entering the rest of the house. The next day a dumpster was positioned underneath the upstairs window to catch the debris. Tom first started on the considerable pile he had made. Throws out the window were easy considering he had the to break up the dry wall small enough to fit through the window. The throwing motion to reach the dumpster resembled that of a Frisbee toss. Albeit, there were definitely some misses. It was easy work for Tom. A crowbar and sledge hammer were the most effective tools used to remove all the dry wall. Within two hours the first night and three more the following day the entire wall and ceiling was removed with a red bandana on over the mouth and nose to seal off any particles. The studs and electrical were now exposed.

Surprisingly, the structure was sound, good old thick oak. Tom finished the second day of remodeling with a shop vac removing the last particles of dust and drywall crumble between studs. The next day's plan was to purchase sheet rock and look for employment as well. Tom and Whit decided to keep the sound electrical in the baby's room.

On this third day in Florida, as with the start of every day, he would first take a whiskey swig and a bubbler rip, but he took an extra one of each this Thursday. To Tom it was in order to loosen himself up for a possible interview. He was able to obtain a couple landscape companies information through the Internet. There was no doubt that a job would be found in this new area with his strong resume, even if it was a petty minimum wage position.

On a seasonably warm April day, three landscape firms would be visited and receive his resume. Next stop, picking up a bottle for the ride home. He concluded the day out with a stop to the hardware store, where he loaded up his child's future walls in the back of his pick up. Upon his arrival back to the shack it was apparent to Whitney that he was drunk as hell. He stumbled through the front door attempting to carry in the sheet rock at four p.m.

"Are you drunk again?"

"I had a couple drinks."

"You're going to be a father soon, what is wrong with you. Why are you always drunk?"

There was a pause. Tom put his head down. "I don't want to be here."

"Why, where do you want to be, where are you going to go? You'd be drunk wherever you are living. Accept your station."

"I know."

Silence would ensue as he unloaded the remainder of the sheet rock from his truck into the baby's room. Whitney ran home and cried to her mom in the office. "He's drunk again... He says the most ridiculous things."

Willy heard the entire conversation in the room over. He got up off his ornamental office chair to peer out toward the shack. "It won't be long till you're gone. Your way or mine."

One of the landscape companies called Tom the following day. Pine Meadows wanted Tom to start immediately. They were thrilled with his interest. Tom thought they were the most interesting of all the companies he applied to. Not only did they specialize in landscape architecture, but they also installed raised bed gardens, vegetable and fruit plants, and irrigation, as well as maintain them. Tom enjoyed the premise. He told them he would start the beginning of the next work week. This brought a little joy to Tom. He now had some means of supporting his family, and new home. Tom was never allowed to touch the savings he had largely contributed to. It was agreed when he was hired that the experienced landscaper would receive a few dollars above minimum wage.

Over the weekend he spent the entirety of the days hanging and taping all the sheet rock. Awareness grew that soon time would be cut short by a full forty-hour work week. He completed the walls and ceilings by Sunday night. Savings were great, especially with Mark sending checks from Hartford. Planning on bringing in someone for the walls, he did it all himself. He started to get nervous while finishing up on Sunday about his first day of work.

Pine Meadows home site was a ten minute drive. He was to be there for seven. The appearance of fourteen men, all in green sweatshirts, huddled around an older man caught Tom's eye Monday morning when he pulled in. The owner, an older gay man named Pat, introduced Tom in front of everyone. Pat gave Tom a brief summary of what Pine Meadows does off site and too what they grow in the greenhouses on the home site. Pat Krause, who began the business thirty years prior, stayed on site growing all the plants that would be brought to the client's property. And too, the owner still worked harder than everyone else at seventy-three.

Tom next met all the guys who made up four separate crews. They were all welcoming. Warm spirited. Most of the men held a similar appearance as that of Tom's- shaggy hair and scruffy face. Tom learned that the men were grouped into crews of two or three under the guidance of one of the three supervisors, each who had there own truck. Trucks, with a Pine Tree logo on the front doors, all carried the same tool collection-rakes, shovels, loppers, trimmers.

Every morning they would meet at the shop in order to go over the assignment for the day. The crew would then load up all the plants from the greenhouse and the building materials necessary for the job. Departure led to hundreds of different accounts, where the larger jobs lasted a couple days. Most plantings and maintenance took only one day, such as weeding, spraying, and pruning. Fine homes, gas stations, small businesses, condos, all employed their labor. Tom's supervisor was Kevin, an older bald man with a narrow head and a gray mustache. Tom's boss seemed to be a very easy-going man.

Owner Pat sent Kevin and his crew to a beautiful estate where they were to plant orange jessamine in already established beds, as well as spread fresh mulch.

The day went quick. Kevin and his two crewmates, Sam and Dave, discussed music and sports for the duration of the day with Tom.

Tom was pleased how the first day went, but he still had his craving right after he punched out in the garage. Sure enough, he got his tonic on the way home. Indeed, painting the baby's room became enjoyable. After showering off the paint, Tom and Whit too had a nice night together. She remained ignorant of what she was certain of. "Lets celebrate your first night of work". Whitney made Tom's favorite dish chicken quesadillas, followed by a movie on the sofa. Whitney, however, could not but feel disgust by the overpowering smell of his breath.

The first days of work into Thursday went very well. Tom was learning a lot about Florida Flora and irrigation. He had never put in irrigation lines before, but he discovered they were very easy. Information mostly was shared by the supervisor, Kevin, who come to find out, was of an environmental mindset similar to

Tom's roommate Mike. He was out there in his opinions. He too felt there was some form of conspiracy by man against nature. "Conspiracy theories will never be institutionally accepted in our society, nobody knows what truly is unraveling!"

This type of person seemed to attract to Tom. Wednesday the crew installed twenty raised beds at an assisted living complex. Kevin held quite a strong opinion on the very vegetable plants they would be planting in the beds.

"People are blind Tom." Kevin spoke these words unexpectedly as he fastened a corner bracket onto two four by fours.

"Huh." Tom did not have any idea what Kevin was trying to say.

"The seeds from most of these plants will not produce new plants; they are infertile. What is going to happen when all vegetables that are grown are producing unproductive seeds? Whose going to control food production? Yes, only the seed company with this patent will have the ability to provide seeds. What will prices become for a simple seed or for food? What about the GMO seeds that research has proven have caused lesions in rats' organs?"

"As I've been collecting seeds for eight years now, I discovered a patent had been awarded in 1998 on a technique that somehow restricts a seed from germinating when planted a second season. I heard of all these new hybrid plants that cannot reproduce and I began to panic. What will happen to the small gardener or farmer. Again with everything else, food is going to be monopolized, which will be controlled at the roots. The large corporations will be in total control. Yes, it's wonderful, man's own intelligence can create a drought resistant or fungal resistant plant, but what in the world is in those seeds to create the ability to avoid a metamorphic event? Will there be any environmental effect?"

"Geez Kev, I never heard of anything like this before."

"You know what's crazier Tom, they are trying to control the weather. You know about the chemtrails?"

"Oh yeah, my roommate Mike made it clear to me."

"Well if they control the conditions of the weather and the seeds, whose going to hold the food supply? The most valuable commodity of all."

Animated conversations of such a high insight, mixed in with sports and music, came to a halt Friday morning. Tom had become a ticking time bomb. Kevin lightly criticized Tom for how high above the ground a butterfly bush's root ball had been planted by the new employee. Tom was hungover. And to make matters worse, he was unable to fix the head pain with the morning ritual, as he was ten minutes late leaving the shack. He did not want to deal with his boss right now. "The plant will grow fine."

"It may, but that is not Pine Meadows quality," Kevin said.

"I've gone to college for this, I know what I'm doing. I don't tell you when I see you doing something incorrect."

"Tom, I'm your boss, you're being pretty disrespectful." Kevin did not want to get into it anymore.

Alcoholism led Tom to feel as if he could blame everyone but himself. Tom then muttered just loud enough for his fifty-year-old boss to hear, "You know nothing."

Kevin immediately responded, "Get in the truck, I'm taking you back to the shop." In the truck, Kevin said a few words while Tom remained silent. "I'm asking you to leave, but you are more than welcome to come back when you wake up sober!"

The potential in Tom was evident. The supervisor could relate to the fight Tom fought day in day out. Kevin Hatcher had been sober from crack and booze for fifteen years, which began in a sober house for six months.

Tom had become blind. No awareness for the positive energy he held. Leaving work, he took the familiar route from the garage to the local bar "The Village". A speed never reached before was performed to reach the imperative destination. He asked for his preferred drink, whiskey on the rocks. Tom got bombed. It is a miracle he made it home safe. Nothing from the bar after the eight heavy jack on the rocks was remembered. At home Whitney could see he was wasted but again. She could not help but cry, both at his weakness and her helplessness. He looked at her, but this time something clicked. He realized the mother of his child was weeping just as he wept on the stairs because of his father.

"I need to leave!"

"Why. What about us? What about the baby? What about the house? What about your job? You need to get help? We can afford it." Whitney was going to pieces.

Tom looked at her with a glum look. Next, a quick quiet pace led him out the door. He jumped in his truck. A quick decision was made to drive twenty-two hours back north. The only place he thought to run was his old home way up north. Still Tom's, but Mark was working on a contract to purchase Tom's house. The money Tom would receive would thus be used on the shack.

Whitney ran after him screaming "Don't go!" which was heard by all those around- Jim, Willy, and Danielle.

About the midway point in Virginia he picked up another handle of whiskey off an exit at a random package store. He didn't open it however, as the lingering drunk sensation kept the entire ride fulfilling the craving. The decision was made to twist it the moment he pulled into his cousin's driveway- making it through with no sleep. Upon arrival, no one was home upstairs. The first floor apartment had not yet been occupied since he and Whitney moved out. The key was still on Tom's key ring. He struggled to fit the key in at eight o' clock in the dark, but with the assistance of a minute of cursing, it finally extended itself in. He turned it, opened the door, and then entered the dark vacant apartment.

Certain unnecessary furniture remained from the time he lived there-couch, coffee table, kitchen table, mattress. Whitney did however remove all of her knickknacks. A sense of emptiness presented itself the moment the owner walked in. With the house now open, Tom walked back to the truck to grab his handle. Brought in, it was set on the coffee table. With two heels in front of the couch, his hind next slammed down into the cushions. Time stood still as he stared at the gallon of whiskey. For a span of twenty minutes Tom's mind unraveled. Conscience foretold there would come a time when he would have to give the partying up. Had the time come? Capable, but he had never even tried. Loudly, he spoke his thought, "Is it going to end?"

Something had to change.

The simple cure for coming down hard from this blackout was an arm's length away. Horizontally, Tom swept his arm across the table grabbing the handle with the strongest of grips. With feet dug into the ground, he then used all his energy into his heels to stand up with the gallon.

A destination for the whiskey to be downed had been set. It was carried outside. Tom found where he wanted to finish off the bottle. A metal lid was removed, which was followed by a violent slam heard round the block. Thousands of glass pieces sat in the bottom of the metal garbage can, along with the potent aroma. Fire water covered Tom, giving off the strongest of odors. But this odor was not the internal odor drunks carry, this odor was much too strong and distinct. This odor was of triumph. Denial never felt so wonderful.

With the genesis of a throbbing headache he went back on the couch, and fell asleep within minutes. Passed out, he didn't see or hear his cousin come in at all. Given the key by Wendy, Mark peeked in while Tom slept at the time his family arrived back from a children's party. Moreover, Tom wanted to avoid his cousin as much as possible. He didn't want to have to explain himself.

The children's noise instantly woke up Tom at six. Around eight, Tom decided to visit upstairs. "Whit and I had a fight." Tom answered all questions in one statement.

A summary was next provided to Mark as to why his cousin left Florida. Mark didn't seem too concerned. Attention seemed to be on his son consuming pancakes. Mark witnessed this ordeal before with his mother. He knew how this would all play out. Mark Jr. didn't let the relatives talk much either though. He just wanted to wrestle with his Uncle Tom. During the wrestling match, which brought Mark Jr. to pin Tom, Tom looked at Mark and told him, "I'm done drinking."

"I hope so," Mark said, "It seems pretty stupid to drive over twenty hours drunk because you had an argument. It's none of my business, but just think of how many times your Dad said he didn't have a problem."

Through some google searches, the time and location of local AA meetings was provided from the computer in Mark's bedroom. Tom was now prepared for humiliation and humbling. Meetings never worked for his father, but he was willing to try. No more options remained. Strangely for him, he felt no urge to drink or smoke subsequent to the decision to find a meeting. He spent a lot of time looking at himself in the mirror that Sunday.

Whitney was lost without Tom. She didn't know what was going to happen- the baby, the house, her life. She didn't want to move back in with her parents. Sympathy would be showered upon her, all because she got pregnant by a deadbeat drunk. She sat as long as she could. A call to Tom's cell phone was made two days after he left. Tom received the call fifteen minutes before his first meeting at seven.

"Hello."

"Tom, we need to talk! I didn't know things were so bad that you had to leave me."

"Whit they are. I have nothing. I put myself in an awful position. I need to figure things out."

"Are we over?" Whit asked.

"I hope not…. Maybe this is just the beginning. I'm going to my first AA meeting tonight."

"Really?"

"Yes, I need to change. I should have listened when everyone said I was a mess."

"Awesome, Tom I need to change too. I need to be more supportive. I know you're under a lot of stress and you have a lot of scars. I always want things my way," Whit said.

"There's no excuse why I'm a drunk, I have to make a choice, either overcome this or just drown. But hun, I have to get going to my meeting for seven."

"OK. I'm proud of you. I love you," Whit said.

"I love you too."

Whitney, through a thirty second phone conversation, changed her mindset completely. She grew optimism, becoming very positive. She knew Tom would find the right path. Even with all the episodes, she never once doubted him or his love. Her father, on the other hand, was certain Tom and Whitney were done. Big Daddy stopped by the shack on the rainy Monday after Tom left.

The one tree Tom bought from the nursery when they first moved in, a Dogwood, was in full pink bloom on this dreary day. It was only ten feet tall, but there seemed to already be hundreds of flowers. Tom, nevertheless, would not see this ornamental tree in its peak.

"Where's Tom?" Willy benevolently asked.

"He had to get help."

"Get help for what," Willy asked.

"Alcohol. His father died from it and he has a problem with it."

"You'll be fine dear, but be prepared. Most drunks will always be drunks"

"I don't think so Dad. I know he'll be back better and stronger, but I really miss him. I wish he was here right now." Tears rolled down Whit's cheeks. "He's not used to all this stress I put on him. You didn't help by pressuring him into marriage. Times are different now. His parents' relationship was a mess."

"I was just busting his chops. What are you going to do about remodeling, I know a guy."

"Give Tom a couple weeks, he will be back," Whit responded.

Willy smiled and walked out. He uttered to himself, "We'll see. Like father, like son."

Tom's first AA meeting was rather moving. He walked down a stairwell into the basement of a bank. As his vision reached the brightly lit lowest level, he saw twenty somber men sitting in a circle. Quiet small conversations spread through the room. However, they all stopped their conversations to glance at Tom. Tom gave a quick smirk, while finding the furthest corner seat away from everyone. All of a sudden the many upbeat side conversations continued.

At the sound of the gavel everyone hushed. The chairperson then commenced the meeting. Grown men being blunt gave Tom such comfort. Everything discussed by each individual could easily be related to, but to Tom there was one thing that immediately stuck. He was allergic to alcohol. "People with allergies may die if they ingest what they are severely allergic to," a clean cut forty-two year old said.

It was as simple as that, the more he would ingest the more he would harm himself- mentally and physically. The man he was sitting next to explained in front of everyone, "If you knew you would burn your hand on an extremely hot stovetop would you put your hand on it?"

Tom didn't say a word at the meeting, but he knew what steps he was to take. He didn't want to burn his soul anymore. Another drink would be destructive. Sobriety was now a matter of life or death. For Tom, success could be possible, all the while he reflected on the example of his father each and every day.

Meanwhile in Florida, Whitney needed to see him, especially now that she knew he was working to fix himself. She wanted to be a part of it. The few days alone were so lonely that she decided a visit was in order. The decision to purchase a one way plane ticket to see Tom on Monday was made. Return would either be provided through flight or on the road with him. The return was up in the air. She thought a road trip home would be great, they could stop anywhere at any time.

She called Tom the minute she arrived at Bradley International Airport, twenty minutes outside of Hartford. Tom jumped in the truck to travel up Ninety-One North. Newspapers, magazines, and books were boring in the old house by this time. Whit's arrival could not come at a better time. A thirty second silent embrace ensued the second Tom got out of the truck to find Whit at the arrival pick-up. Whitney instantly spoke, "Come back Tom. I need you. Our child will need you. You can never do this to me again!"

A visit to their old bare apartment was the next stop, but the excitement to simply see Tom was most overwhelming. It was only four days after he left, but he began to feel change. The two meetings he attended Sunday and Monday were already improving his mental state. He now knew he had to fix his mind.

Tom had been rehearsing the extensive lot of things he had to say. "OK. I now know if we are to last I must be sober. Everything I have done drunk has been false. Something foreign was controlling my actions. I will find meetings down there. I was a drunk mess the other night I had no control. I'm sorry! Soon I will be in full control of my reality. I will never step even a pinky toe outside of it. I don't know if I will finish the house before the baby, but I will try my hardest. Just be patient give me time. The meetings here are so intense. It's a great group of guys."

"OK," Whitney said.

Whitney flew home Wednesday happy as can be. Tom wanted to spend one more week with his AA group. Whitney would first visit the mansion the moment she pulled in the Sunny Side entrance. She told her parents of Tom's improvement. "He's sober and he's coming back."

Tom made it back into Florida on the following tuesday.

The first family dinner with Tom back was quite awkward even for Uncle Jim. He didn't say much. All Willy spoke of was a huge marketing opportunity at the Tallahassee Convention Center, in which Sunny Side could purchase a weekend booth at the National Time

Share Show. Quality marketing could serve as the best tool to fill all the new slots available in the new construction. It was the best way to share the brochures for the new and old condos with thousands of interested consumers. Of the few things Tom spoke in front of Whit's family, he unexpectedly said, "I'll do it for you. I owe you for the house!" Best of all, Big Willy didn't have to pay a dollar for Tom's labor.

All Uncle Jim said on the matter was, "Why bother?"

Tom's issues didn't come up at all.

Big Willy pretended to be happy. However, he and Jim later stepped foot in the grounds garage. First, as always, they got to talking about the mowers and tractors. Nevertheless, Tom quickly came up. Consideration would be shared for staking out the shack. To catch Tom in an ill condition would verify their assumptions. Uncle Jim even brought up the idea to pay a private investigator to follow him. They were certain he would always be a drunk punk.

"Jim, remember that security contractor that came by a couple months back inquiring about contracting the new development."

"Yep," Jim said.

"Well, I think it's the right time to get some estimates. I won't sleep right if I got some no good drunk living in my back yard; doing lord knows what. I need to find out who he really is."

"Do it up, I don't want scum here either," Jim said.

The two then said cheers, and chugged the last two on the top half of the thirty pack.

"Where is the crew working today?" Willy asked Jim regarding the four Guatemalans.

"Outside of eight, they're planting some gazanias and mulching. I asked them to join us. They should be here anytime." Jim looked at his watch.

The two discussed the torn belt on the z-turn for a minute before the four Guatemalan's walked in. They were all smiles, as they knew cold beers awaited, rather than work in the heat.

"Come grab one." Willy said. He didn't have much communication with them compared to Jim.

"Sure," said Salou, as the only one in the crew that could speak and understand English. He told the others to grab their drinks.

"Salou, what do you think of Whitney's guy?" Willy asked.

"I don't say much to him," answered Salou.

"He's no good," Jim said.

"You guys mind keeping an eye on him at night? We'll pay you in cash, just don't tell anyone where you're getting the money. Jim will sacrifice and work some of your hours, so you can switch off and get some sleep. Sound good?" Willy asked.

Salou looked at the three, spoke ten words, and then nodded his head up and down. One of the crew spoke some words to Salou.

"Hmmm. Willy, do you want to put some magic on him. We can make spells. Make him go away," Salou said.

"Yes, anything. I don't believe in your voodoo, but if you're magic will get him off my land, do it!"

The six finished their beers. Jim then said the dreaded phrase, "Back to work."

Willy then went to the office in hopes of recovering the business card of the intriguing security firm. The instant he found it he called. The Continental Security Agency (CSA) was now to be in business with Sunny Side Condos. Willy had always wanted surveillance, but he was going to wait until the new condos were up. Since Tom arrived, however, Willy had been uneasy. Uncle Jim made the call to CSA. The call described his interest to install security in portions of the existing Sunny Side community immediately. "There is a suspicious tenant I want to catch."

The two parties reached an agreement the following day. Two days later, CSA immediately showed up equipped for installation. The exterior security cameras and voice monitor speakers were set up with Tom and Whitney home. Willy told Whitney all the work was for telecommunication and Internet purposes. Cameras and microphones were mounted on tree and telephone poles around the entire exterior of the shack. Every device was undetectable by the naked eye.

Willy also turned to fear mongering upon Tom's return. More often than not, when Tom was home in the evenings or on the weekend, Willy would take out a piece from the showcase to have some target practice. There was a large border of Pine trees that muffled the sound from the condos, but to Tom the shots were fired right in his front yard. Tom, on the other hand, was going to kill Willy with kindness. He didn't care what kind of guns his father-in-law owned.

Tom waved Willy down on one of his shooting sprees. He walked over to the large man when the gun was put down. "I'll do that time-share convention for you," Tom said.

This motion made Willy uneasy. "Really, Why?"

"Well Willy, you letting me work on the shack is a kind gesture and I would like to return it."

"Sure, I'll have Danielle get you all the info."

The thing that bothered Tom most, however, was the lack of trust or respect Willy and Jim had for him. There was not one bad thing Tom had ever done to either of them, but say some mean things he didn't know he was saying to Whitney. Whit was the closet thing to Tom. Of course she was going to see him at his weakest.

He cleaned himself up in order to give Whitney the best life available. However, he would never do right in Jim or Willy's eyes. Tom was well aware he made a mess, but now he began to clean it all up. With all the paranoia and suspicion that the two had formed upon Tom, he still continued to improve his spirit. Treatment toward the two haters would be filled with kindness. He clearly knew what Willy and Jim were trying to do.

Fortunately, Tom got his landscape job right back. It was a simple phone call that fixed everything between Kevin and Tom. He called Kevin personally and told him the truth, "I am an alcoholic and you saw me at my lowest. I apologize, you didn't deserve any of that Kev."

"I knew the moment I met you Tom that you were one of us. No worries, most of the crew can relate. Tom, come back and give Pine meadows another shot when you're ready. We'll erase that Friday"

Thus Kevin would soon sponsor Tom after the phone call.

Every night after work Tom continued to work on the remodeling, yet still saving time for Whit- lower backrubs, foot rubs, trips to the store for ice cream and pickles. Most importantly though he was continually working on himself- attending afternoon meetings immediately after work everyday, working on the twelve steps. Even with the tension Sunny Side provided, things were getting stronger between the young couple. Indeed, Tom had to strengthen himself. Willy, nonetheless, was getting mighty jealous. Even if Tom was a Nobel peace prizewinner, Willy would still want him gone.

Willy went as far as contacting the mob he had used in the past to get tenants to pay their overdue rent. He told the head guy John that if anything popped up through surveillance they were on speed dial. Willy also asked his head of the mob friend if he could have someone sit in on these "alcoholic meetings" Tom attended.

"No problem," John told Willy on the phone, "I will send my big guy, 6'3" two fifty to attend. If he hears anything out of line or defiling to your family he'll be done immediately."

Ironically, the man sent by John for Willy named TJ had some bad habits himself. The more TJ attended the meetings, sitting alongside Tom, the more he went for himself rather than Tom. One meeting he came clean confessing about getting paid to beat people up, he didn't mention the situation with Tom though. Tears fell because of his past in front of fifteen grown men. TJ however told John another story after every meeting, in which TJ told John that Willy had nothing to worry about. Tom knew nothing of what Willy set-up.

Uncle Jim, on the other hand, was in on everything Willy was administering. Willy told him at break, "I don't care if he's going to be my grandson's father, he is scum. I'm going to treat him like the punk he is. Whitney's still young and dumb."

"Well boss, you got to do what you got to do. Everything you've done thus far has worked just perfect for you."

Salou, the head Guatemalan, made a deal with Jim that the crew would help Tom with his plantings around the shack in order to see if he was still drinking. Intrigue also lingered as to what his posture toward Willy and Jim was.

"Tom we will help you," Salou said.

"Really, you don't have to."

"No man, we watch you work very hard everyday."

"I'm just planting some boxwoods today."

"Easy man." Salou and the crew began to take the pots off and open the root ball.

"You guys sure you don't want to relax. You work so hard being so far away from your family. I don't know how you do it."

"Don't worry about us."

In a half hour of labor the boxwoods were all planted. Tom felt awful he did not have any cash or booze on hand to share with the Guatemalan's for their labor. However, the crew made it very clear that they wanted nothing in return. Little did Tom know the

Guatemalan's purpose was to find an object of Tom's. They were educated in spirituality and rites from their homeland. Manipulation of words and objects gave a trained practitioner the ability to cripple, even kill, a person under the spell. The most important element for Salou and his crew to cast a spell was that the subject must have a blocked energy chord, which when free would connect the subject to their highest spiritual state. If the sorcerer can discover what event or obsession spoils the pure spirit, then witchcraft will prevail. In many cases for Salou, all it would take to disrupt the mind was a simple word that brings uneasiness. Salou chose an item of Tom's to curse, wherein he grabbed a work glove of Tom's that was left outside. Nothing worked, however, Tom focused his energy on repairing his damaged soul in order to navigate his spirit toward the correct direction.

Willy and Jim steadfastly worked on making Tom feel unwelcomed. Quite often, Tom would bring home ill garbage shrubs from work to plant around his house. Albeit, Jim and Willy would take turns driving by at different times in order to give Tom the look of death. Jim would mutter just loud enough for Tom to hear.

"Man, he's wasting his time, planting on someone else's land" or "Why is he planting that all it looks like crap." or "What's he thinking?" or "It's all Willy's property."

Tom ignored it all. His philosophy stood the ground that nothing stays constant in this universe. Things either improve or diminish. He knew if he did the right thing every moment of the day, his life would gradually improve. He wouldn't be provoked into any ill reaction.

On the subject of the fear-mongering Willy Stanton, Tom had become fearless. He said confidentially to his sponsor Kevin at work, "They are able to control everything outside, but inside they have no control over me. I am discovering the person I truly am and they are no part. And I am a good man, others make me out to be bad, but it is them who are truly evil. They are viewing themselves through me. I must pray they improve."

Change

Two months of surveillance had been placed on Tom, even as he lived clean as a whistle and pumping his life savings into the same man's land who was spying on him. At least one Guatemalan watched the shack every night with Jim's night vision binoculars from the wood line.

Willy had every second of site and sound surveillance available on his computer. However, there was nothing done by Tom that would give Willy justification to rid the recovering alcoholic out of Whitney's life. The baby was a few weeks away. The house was almost finished. Tom had learned so much. The reward for bringing over several contractors he met through work. Men who knew plumbing, electrical, carpentry, A.C., were more than happy to share free advice to Tom. He didn't invest much money into labor, but he did spend a lot on materials.

A little over a week before the baby was born Tom agreed to represent 'Sunny Side Condo's' at the time-share convention. Whit designed all the catalogues, brochures, and laminated offerings, which Tom presented on two tables. The young man who looked very professional and welcoming wore a yellow dress shirt with a blue and yellow tie- attractive but not flashy.

His approach was simple. He smiled at everyone that looked over at the booth. For the thousands that came over, he found an ice breaking common subject, which served as the means to introduce Sunny Side. The locals that attended loved the fact that Willy's future son-in-law was helping him out, and also, that such a wonderful boy was blessing the Stanton's with their first grandchild.

The weekend went great. Tom was very kind and welcoming to everyone. He talked with near ten thousand people during the two eight hour days-handing out every single pamphlet Whit had created. The new condos were set to open in less than a year. If they were filled before construction was finished, Willy would look brilliant. A large increase in his bank account would transpire.

The one downer for Tom was Jim's visit. Tom spotted Uncle Jim amid the crowd about fifteen feet from the booth. He gave Tom the nastiest look ever. Didn't even say a word as he walked by. Tom thought to himself, "The audacity of that fool, I'm here donating my weekend for free to pay his future salary. What an ungrateful disgrace." One other Sunny Side family member showed up. Whitney stopped by and joined

Tom for an hour. She made it clear to the possible consumers that she was the owner's daughter. And boy did she bring in big business for that daddy of hers in an hours time. It was a no brainer. Potential clients saw the owner's daughter, who lived on the grounds, pregnant.

Sure enough, the week following the convention, Danielle received eight hundred calls regarding the new condos. Within two weeks, the new condos were filled completely, all because of Tom's free labor. This was the first time interested patrons were ever put on a waiting list for Sunny Side.

Uncle Jim did not see it this way. "That fucking punk better work his ass off for you. He owes you a lot of money for letting him redo that shack."

On a usual Thursday for Uncle Jim it was the same routine. Early on in the day he checks all the plant beds and, if need be, draws up plans for future plantings. He then finishes up early at two, compared to the other days when he oversees the mowing and weed prevention until four. The after work local venue was the same as every other Thursday-The Village Tavern. All other nights out were spent at the Gentlemen's Club. It had been Uncle Jim's destination for ten years now and was special- a night without flinging dollar bills. It was the closest watering hole, with a refined character.

Jim knew everyone, from the owner, to the bus boy, to the divorcee sitting alone by the window. On this Thursday he would meet someone he didn't recognize, but who still would change his mind forever. Jim was the type to engage in conversation with any new face, as long as he had been inspired by at least one cocktail.

Uncle Jim may be considered an alcoholic by most standards. He had at least three alcoholic beverages daily, but he was nowhere near the range of Tom's prior daily binges. Thursday's were the only time Jim would truly get drunk. This was a Thursday Jim planned on having a few extra drinks. There was a buzz out about Sunny Side. An article in the local paper described the swift construction for the units already filled. Everyone wanted to talk to Jim about the amazing progress. But most important, his job was set in stone, in fact the expansion of Sunny Side brought on promotion. The success also led Jim to perceive his taking over as the most likely scenario. The Sunny Side system was formed just as much by Jimmy as it was by Willy.

The furthest stool to the right was going to be his spot for the duration of daylight. It always was. This day was different. He noticed a gentleman sitting on a center stool. A man with overgrown white hair and a long white beard, shaven under the chin line, was the lone soul at the barside. He was dressed in khaki shorts with a vibrant Hawaiian shirt.

Jim immediately sat next to him in his clean work khaki's and black Sunny Side polo. Jim made an obvious up and down look. "First time in the Village?"

"Yes, nice and quiet." The man returned the look.

"I come here on Thursdays to throw a couple back. I'm pretty flat out this time of year, but I always save time for the Village."

"What do you do?"

"I'm head groundskeeper, maintenance man, and landscape architect at Sunny Side Condo's. My name is Jim by the way."

"I'm David Meyers. Please to meet you. I've read a little about that place."

"Yeah. We're expanding, doubling our size. Everything has gone through nice and smooth so far, except for one issue. I can't wait to start designing."

"Sounds great. Who do you have for security?"

"Continental Security Agency. Their great you know, get things done real fast. They first contacted the owner of the condo's, Willy Stanton. He's my best friend as far back as childhood. We grew up together all the way through. Lately, he's had a lot of trouble with his no good punk son-in-law." Jim had a chuckle. "That's why we got the security, not for any other reason. This kid is an ugly drunk. Before this kid Tom came and lived in the condos for free, cause he wasn't worth a dime, we didn't have any security. The second he came in though,

Willy saw his girl crying. Sure enough, we had an eye on his place the whole time since. Willy can watch the house from his computer. He also can hear any conversation in the house. Kid don't have a clue. Willy ain't worried cause it's all Willy's property, everything is his on paper. Kid put thousands of dollars into this shack, actually looks great, but it don't matter, his name ain't on nothing."

"Wow, kid don't know a thing huh. What's sweat equity right." David seemed very interested in Jim's boasting.

"I never trusted him for a second. We even monitor his bank account. It's fine cause it started out as Whitney's, which Willy started up for her to receive money for college. Apparently, this kid Tom loads all his money in there. We see every deposit and card transaction made. Thing is he sobered up for a couple months now and he don't buy booze anymore. Nor does the relationship seem dysfunctional. We're going to continue to check on him, make sure things don't turn wrong." Jim chuckled again, "Willy has the mob on speed dial. He had them watch his house and take a photo of Tom and his vehicle to make sure they knew who to hit." ... "Enough about what's going on with me. Want a drink? What do you do?"

"I'm fine for now, gotta finish my red wine. Well, it's funny you ask. I'm in security as well. That's why I asked you." David saw Jim's eyes light up with the acknowledgment of his occupation.

"Well, we have a lot in common. What's the name of your firm?"

"Actually Jim I like to think of myself as a people's servant. Security for the people. Someone has to look out for the common man."

"What?" Jumped out of Jim's mouth.

"Yes, I am an attorney for civil liberties. There are a lot of whistle blowers for domestic spying."

"You work for the feds?" Jim asked.

"I somewhat work against the feds nowadays. Too many government officials are looking out for their own invested interest not the peoples. I'm trying to make sure things are fair."

"Huh." Jim held a puzzled look.

"Everything you have disclosed to me Jim sounds illegal. You won't believe it but to me you're supporting terrorism. You're taking someone's freedom away by your sneaky measures. The private company that you contracted for security is an American based private company who the government outsources abroad. All those recordings that Tom is unaware of are received by the main cloud and stored accordingly by the Federal Investigation Agency (FIA). Do you realize the true purpose is to analyze information that could possibly disrupt the growth of our corporate monopolies."

"What the hell are you talking about Dave. I just want to shoot the breeze and have a couple drinks. ... But you know as well as I do, we are in a time of war. Different rules do apply."

"Listen Jim I know all this. I worked in the Federal Investigation Agency for twenty years. I know the games they play. They can do whatever they want. But what happens if a war last forever? Must we permanently commit illegal acts? Must we censure permanently? Must we invade foreign countries, form new laws, form new wars? Incessant warfare has become the norm. This violent nature is worshipped here."

"I don't give two shits about foreigners. I belong to the greatest nation in the world."

"Ah Jim. The moral superiority complex. Let me ask you, of what virtues we hold make us the center of the universe? Do you act in accordance with your ego or your spirit?"

"Man, Dave, don't you know how to have a good time."

"Jim, I would be having a much better life if I knew there was a concern by our government to spare innocent lives no matter what country they live."

"My life is good here Dave, I work hard and pay my bills. I'm not worried about over there."

"It's all connected. Our taxes are supporting a war the majority of taxpayers didn't support. You are also paying for the unknowing surveillance upon American taxpayers."

"David, what's the big deal. If someone isn't committing wrong why should they care to be monitored?"

"It's wrong!" David raised his tone.

There stood an awkward silence.

"I agree Dave this war does cost a lot of money." Jim wanted to bring Dave back to a pleasant mood.

"Well Jim, as we're fighting this war for our freedom, we are truly losing it."

"I never looked at it like that," Jim said.

"Think of it this way Jim. Take a little boy who was very tall and skinny. His parents only had one type of mirror throughout the house. This mirror was the only means by which the child ever saw his reflection. Unfortunately, this mirror was the type to be found in the circus, which makes the thin and tall appear fat and short. This boy would go on to think he was obese, growing up under this perception. Well Jim, we have been deceived like this boy. We need to see the natural reflection. 'War is terrorism.'[ix] You've supported every bombing that has killed so many innocent lives."

"I see what you're getting at Dave. Go on."

"Politics and the media can exhibit any picture they want to the public. We the people are so blind to this." Dave then ranted, "Who is the government truly for nowadays- people or corporations? What the fuck is national security? Making every other nation hate us because of our dependence on oil and the deeds we commit to obtain it sure helps our security. Thanks a lot Washington for the lack of preparation for the ensuing energy crisis!"

"What if our way of life, also identified to be our national security, is wrong? It is destroying this earth! It is forming hatred exponentially!"

"The government and the people are two very different entities. The American illusion allows us to believe we are one family, yet the rich and the working class are far different people. Why would the working class think invading a foreign country is in its best interest if taxes would intensely be increased? The politicians claim war is in the nations best interest yet the taxes still increase. The division of classes is the true struggle within this nation. One small group feels the necessity to make decisions for the larger poor group. The poor group has no property or money. Thus the lesser group has no opportunity to improve living standards. Ha, we want to fix out there." Dave spun on the stool pointing his index fingers every which way. He then pointed both fingers at himself. "We need to fix within before we move outside."

"How old is that kid you're spying on?"

"Twenty-four or five I think." Jim quickly responded in a light embarrassed tone.

"He's a kid. What were you doing at that age? People polarize everything nowadays. He's cleaned himself up. Give him some credit. Maybe he comes from a broken home, his dad was probably a drunk…"

"He was," Jim chimed in.

"That's the only manner he knew how to deal with problems or nerves. That kid might solve all these problems I've been complaining about someday. You can't assume you know what someone's going to do," Dave said.

"Yes. I suppose it's like this war Dave. Not all these foreigners are terrorists."

"Exactly Jim. There are so many innocent victims in this war on ignorance. The soldiers' intentions are for the best interest of the country, which ironically forms a greater impossible debt for our decorated citizens to return to. Money is not being used wisely. It should be spent on energy infrastructure. That is where the answer will be found. These power lines are not going to last. Oil is not going to last."

"I think you're wrong about that Dave."

"Insane profits for private military contractors are one of the many distresses formed by the corporate control of vital resources." Dave finished his wine, cleaned his lips with a napkin, and continued. "It is true the constitution enables this. Similar to the bible, its words can have multiple interpretations.[x] Why should we fight and grow in debt for a small portion of men who are protecting their interest. When we won the revolution Jim, the whole country did not gain independence. Slaveholders, merchants, and manufacturers benefited from our separation from Britain, the petty man still had to pay off universal debts. One with wealth, as long as their not a jester of the lowest standard, will have no problem maintaining their wealth. The wealthy in society have been able to continue the status-quo through these hundred of years controlling the nation through one class. The ruling class has known that bringing about war was the best way to accomplish subjection. The lower class had to both fight the battles and pay the debt."

"Dave let me buy you another drink. I see your passion. I really like what your saying. ... Knowledge is power. I want to live by the truth."

The two waited as the bartender poured them each a gin and tonic on the rocks.

"Dave, I always have been into war you know. That's why this talk is hard for me. I've watched all those movies. Now thinking about it, maybe those movies are used as a promotional tool."

"Exactly Jim. Only certain events are promoted, but even these are manipulated. If a conflict arises, the delinquency requires intervention in order to justify our involvement. Speculation forms through various means in order to make violence the only solution. Propaganda fills the mind with all the justification necessary to support even the most immoral of all acts. These political parties are a farce. They both produce the same end. The American people are not truly represented, yet we invade the homeland of millions in our name... 'Nothing justifies killing innocent people'[xi]."

"This makes me wonder who the real terrorist are Dave? This is troubling. The most important matters seem to be hidden," Jim said.

"You hit the nail on the head. Losing thousands during a terror act is absolute devastation. However, how many innocent people have we killed? We do not have to face any consequence for murder by our machines."

"But there is no solution, right Dave?"

"Well, if the government becomes destructive to our life, liberty, and pursuit of happiness, the people have the right to alter and abolish it. I'm sure not happy with what's been going on. If anyone corrupts the truth, they are wrong. I don't care who they are. ... Patriotism isn't full support for the government, what if their guilty. In consideration that many men are driven by greed, what if some of those men are our rulers? Are we supposed to keep our mouth shut and allow one man to take what another man is due?"

"Dissent is as important an element of patriotism as compliance. This nation grew great wealth from slaves not too long ago, but men existed who knew it was wrong and persevered to end it. We must focus on humanics rather than war and selfishness. The solution to this mess will never form through occupation in lands we have no knowledge of. We must have debates based on facts and logic. The truth holds a supremacy no propaganda could imitate."

It was now seven o' clock. The two enjoyed each other's company by this time, even though the tab piled up so high that some of the conversation was to be lost. Jim did not want the night to end, nor did David.

"Jim do you know what Mark Twain wrote once:

'The gospel of the monarchical patriotism is 'The King can do no wrong'. We have adopted it with all its servility, with an unimportant change in the wording: 'Our country, right or wrong!' We have thrown away the most valuable asset we had-the individual's right to oppose both flag and country

when he believed them to be in the wrong. We have thrown it away,' and with it, all that was really respectable about that grotesque and laughable word; Patriotism.'[xii]"

Jim quickly said, "He was a smart man."

"Before we depart, do you want me to tell you how we really got into this mess of a war?"

"Of course Dave. Please educate me."

Anglo-Iran

"So Jim, what do think made the mid-east hate us?
Why did Iran take hostages from the US embassy? ... A
grave upheaval occurred, which permanently separated
the two nations. American had actually disrupted the
growth of democratic Iran. A coup was formed by
American and British interests in order to obtain vast
oil. We destroyed Iran's movement toward social
equality."

"There is such a lack of facts Americans hold on our foreign affairs. We feel we are always in the right. Yet we never know the entire story. Our history is 375 years old. The histories of the middle-eastern countries span thousands of years. The past is truly celebrated. Known by those who remain passionate for their country. Iran, also known as Persia, had an ocean of oil beneath its ground, which would generate great interest in the beginning of the twentieth century. However, this would cause more harm than good within Iran. A terrible mess for the Iranian working class would form."

"A treaty was signed in 1907 that split Iran between two European powers-Russia and Britain. Britain gained the south, while Russia gained the north. Russia didn't hold much opportunity to expand in Iran though. They were caught in both a civil war and revolution. Britain, on the other hand, held significant power. And at this point oil became one of Britain's greatest interests. You know as well as I do, oil is more of a necessity than gold."

"In 1901 before any treaty was formed an agreement was reached between 'a self-taught geologists' named George Reynolds from London and the Shah of Iran. Reynolds had the exclusive right to search for oil. The shah was guaranteed 20,000 pounds, an equal amount in shares of the company, and a promise of 16 percent of future profits."

"The finances would ultimately be provided by the Burmah Oil Company based out of Glasgow. It was a monumental agreement as fossil fuels would soon become the largest used substance for energy. Hence, it made the British seek Iranian occupancy. It was clear that whoever held the oil held dominance throughout the world. The only catch was to discover it."

"By 1908, with the discovery of oil fields, investors formed the Anglo-Persian Oil Company, which developed oil exploration and refineries. Five years later the British government bought 51 percent of the company for two million pounds. Thus, the Anglo-Persian Company immediately began laying hundreds of miles of pipeline and drilling wells within its first years. Millions of barrels were being produced and then sent out to filling stations throughout England. Iranian oil would be sold throughout Europe and Australia."

"Success brought establishment. The British employees built wonderful homes and landscapes within the refineries region. The Iranians, however, continued to live in the slums. It was colonial segregation. All western amenities were off limits to the very Iranian men laboring to increase the profit for the British. Lord Curzon described the effects of oil control pertaining to World War I: 'the allies floated to victory on a wave of oil'. Moreover, the royal navy received its oil at a much reduced price."

"The Anglo-Persian Oil Co. continued to grow and produce more oil while the profits continually increased, in which Iranian's slowly began to question their 16 percent share. The Iranians were dubious- not allowed to look at the books or audit the thriving enterprise. In 1928, the comparison of living conditions between the British and the Iranians was vastly different, hence, the ruling Shah wished to change the status Iran held with the oil company. The British company, nevertheless, would simply refuse. Royalties received by the Iranians would actually decrease. A deal was finally settled in 1933, in which concessions were made which lasted until 1961. The name of the company would be changed to the Anglo-Iranian Company. The British, however, would impose the removal of Iranian leader Reza Shah eight years after the agreement. The oil company would still greatly benefit from oil without granting greater concessions for Iran."

"In 1941 six and a half million tons was extracted and by 1945 sixteen and a half million tons was extracted. In 1946 the Iranian workers became crestfallen. They went on strike, angered by poor living conditions and minimal wages. The British still didn't care and chose not to negotiate. Men died through the violence of rioting. Eventually, the oil company agreed to follow Iran's labor laws. However, actions are much greater than words, and the British claims were never fulfilled."

"The British decided to threaten Iranian safety as a result of the internal dissent. They would place two warships within the view of the refinery. The lack of improvement for conditions oppressed the Iranians in their own land. A law was passed in 1947 by the Iranian parliament requiring a renegotiation of the deal made between Anglo-Iran and Iran. The man who wrote this bill was named Mohammad Mossadegh. The Shah had previously kicked Mossadegh out of Iranian politics, but with the Shah's departure he was back planting the seed for a confrontation of enormous proportions. He felt no one foreign entity held jurisdiction in Iran over an Iranian. Iran was being screwed."

"In 1947 the company earned forty million pounds and gave Iran seven million. There was no trust in the British Company, but the British continued to feel entitled. They had built and developed all the refineries.

Iran would not collect any compensation due according with the 1933 agreement. Workers were still only paid fifty cents a day. The Anglo-Iranian company would continue to not consider any compromise to benefit the Iranian people. The British had now risen to world power through the excessive use of others' resources, as the case of Iran clearly illustrated."

"Mossadegh wanted change immediately. Subsequent to an election filled with fraud, he marched thousands to the royal palace from his home. He refused to move until the Shah held fair elections. Through this defiance a formation of several groups arose which favored a democratic Iran, with less influence from outside companies. Mossadegh and other members of this new group known as the National Front were soon elected. A new political landscape would now form within Iran. Mossadegh would eventually become the Iranian Prime Minister following many efforts to nationalize the oil industry, which in turn won over most Iranians. Mossadegh was a far different prime minister from those that had previously served. Those that served prior had held little power, as the Shah had called all the shots."

"Mossadegh viewed the oil conflict as a struggle for Iran's independence. Thus he would lead the Iranian government into debates never once considered. Conflict was stirring, soon to become inevitable. Nationalizing the Anglo-Iranian Oil Company was atop all priorities for the prime minister. This defiance led Mossadegh to be viewed as a national hero. Yet the British still held no interest in compromise, using threats of an invasion by troops if opposition continued. The British strongly felt they had the legal right to distribute Iranian oil, because they constructed everything necessary to produce the oil. The oil company would even reduce their payment to Iranian workers. As a result, thousands left their work post in protest. Fights and deaths broke out between the British and Iranians. War ships continued to remain within sight of the refinery. It was becoming a huge mess over there."

"America remained neutral in their policy towards Iran. We were actually viewed favorably by the Iranians. They thought we were the great nation that successfully revolted against colonialism. There were many Americans, also, who dedicated their time for the improvement of Iran. President Truman also supported Iran and wanted to help the underdeveloped nation. Many within the United States and British government, however, feared the role Russia would play in Iran. The end of World War II brought on communism as the great dynamic that would doom the United States. If Iran would align their oil with Russia the west would reap dire consequence. Therefore, in 1947 the CIA was formed with President Truman's approval during these international uncertainties."

"The British, on the other hand, were baffled as to why Truman refused to support the development Britain had formed in Iran. Iranians could not have solely created any of what Britain had formed, yet consequently, under the matter of jurisdiction the Iranians would successfully vote to nationalize their oil.

The British argued that if Iran nationalized its oil, the west's cost of living would increase, but more importantly, the Russians would greatly increase their power. In 1951 Mohammad Reza Shah signed a law removing the deal with Anglo-Iran. The National Iranian Oil Company would be established to take its place. Multiple minimal settlements were attempted on paper by the British toward Iran, but none were satisfactory to the nation atop an ocean of oil. Iran wanted sovereignty for their own natural resource."

"A great insult occurred when Mossadegh brought in his own to extract the oil- a fellow Iranian was to act as managing director of the National Oil Company. When the director arrived at the running refinery, he declared himself boss over the British employees. His first priority was the request of receipts from every tanker, which would show the Iranians how much was being exported. The British, however, would not succumb to this measure. The oil legally belonged to Anglo-Iran.

Demands for the receipts would be denied, while tanker captains were told by Britain to pump all the oil out of the holds, leaving the Iranian oil supply drained. The next step for the British was to remove all their employees out of Iran, but when the British left they left behind incriminating paperwork. It was revealed that the Anglo-Iranian Oil Company had influentially won over Iranian parliament members. Newspapers too were used to make false allegations. The Iranian government shared all the revelations publicly. The British were left with one option. They now sought to overthrow Mossadegh."

"The U.S. didn't favor Britain, but they didn't favor Iran. This made Mossadegh mad, he felt the U.S. was ignoring the injustice the Iranians faced. Furthermore, Iran faced another problem. There was no one that was trained for senior administration or field technician, nor did they have any tankers to export the oil. Still, none of this bothered Mossadegh. He felt this was Iran's time for liberation. There were no deals to be made as the British ministers were so distant from Iranian's needs. The only time ministers had previously visited Iran was for issues of war, not once had any minister considered to inspect workers rights. Iranians were now prepared to sacrifice oil in order to rid British colonialism. Storage tanks were full of oil, yet the captains were advised not to fill up their tankers in 1951. The British ships also set up blockades to eliminate other European ships benefitting from Iranian oil. The Iranians had stalled the great enterprise of Britain, but Britain would stall progress for Iran."

"Mossadegh addressed the United Nations in 1951:

'My countrymen lack the bare necessities of existence. Their standards of living is probably one of the lowest in the world. Our greatest asset is oil. This should be the source of work and food for the population of Iran. (...) The petroleum industry has

*contributed practically nothing to the well-being of
the people or to the technical progress or industrial
development of my country'."*

"The American government recognized that the
Iranian Prime Minister was fully supported by the mass
population in Iran. They also felt he was honest and well
educated- he studied in Paris and Switzerland. The
British, adversely, defined him as a crazy fanatic.
Consequently, Mossadegh's denial of Anglo-Iran was
punishing for Iran's economy. Everyday got worse. He
received no support from Truman or even the World
Bank in 1952. Iran earned forty-five million from oil in
1950 and in 1952 they received next to nothing. The
British had one option left to salvage their refinery. An
overthrow of Mossadegh would be the only solution.
Agents decided to set up a coup to rid Mossadegh, who,
through informants, heard of this plot. As a result, on
October 16th he broke diplomatic relations with Britain,

ridding all British diplomats from Iran by the end of the month."

"Fortunately for the British, a new presidential election in America was on the horizon. Truman wasn't running for reelection. Dwight Eisenhower would be elected as Truman's replacement. Hence, the British focused now on Eisenhower and his possible influence in Iran. During and following the election the CIA had a gentleman named Kermit Roosevelt in Tehran running the organization's Middle East operations. He was also the grandson to former President Theodore Roosevelt."

"Kermit Roosevelt left Tehran for home a little after the American election. Before home, Kermit first stopped in London. He met with friends in the Secret Intelligence Service. They told Kermit they were extremely interested in overthrowing Mossadegh. Roosevelt, additionally, had a feeling the new administration may think contrary to Truman on Iran. The key for Roosevelt to have success upon his return to Iran would be through the role internal Iranian agents would play. The British had established quite a large number of Iranian dissidents over the years and Roosevelt would have complete access to them."

"Two weeks after Eisenhower was elected, British Intelligence met the CIA in Washington. A plan to pay Iranian mob leaders to develop hysteria in Tehran was erected, which would ultimately lead to Mossadegh's arrest. An American Ambassador would also contact many Iranian's who seemed interested in removing Mossadegh. Americans no longer felt a deal could be made between Iran and Britain, in which high-level officials felt the best means to avoid a communist Iran would be to overthrow the government. The CIA now declared war on Mossadegh. It was a declaration that would be unknown to the common man for decades. The pot began to be stirred. The most potent ingredient was an internal mob."

"In sermons, on street corners, in newspapers, the CIA infiltrated the culture through bribery and other means. An anti-Mossadegh ideology had arisen and was quickly spreading. It was fertile ground to plant the seed of revolt in. Mossadegh had driven away Iran's most influential money-maker, and consequently, a mob was organized and headed straight toward Mossadegh's house. His front gate was broke into. Mossadegh had no choice but to flee over a garden wall. This event showed the CIA that the removal of Mossadegh was possible. Thus the CIA administration in Washington transferred one million dollars to Tehran for the agents participating in the affair. They were to use the money by any means to achieve the removal of Mossadegh."

"Americans were now plotting against pro-democratic Iran. Mossadegh had no idea. He wrote a letter to Eisenhower describing Iran's financial and political hardships. Eisenhower didn't respond for a month. When he finally did the president recommended that Iran repair the situation with Britain. Eisenhower would grow blind to the chain of events once he approved the coup plot."

"Thugs were receiving money to attack religious figures with the claim that Mossadegh authorized it. Public opinion was being manipulated through articles written in Washington and then published in Iran. Alongside religious men pleading for Mossadegh's removal, demonstrations had arisen because of provoking newspaper articles. Agents were spread throughout Tehran. The angry mob became the most valuable of tools for the prime minister's removal. The next step was to capture Mossadegh."

"Iranian operatives could make the end possible. Some were flown into CIA headquarters in Washington for training. They were the ones who first planted the seed for anti-Mossadegh views. The time to reap the harvest would be near. They organized propaganda, sabotaged media, and formed riots. To finally end Mossadegh's reign, Roosevelt had his agents spread a story that Mossadegh had tried to overthrow the Shah and take his position. Corrupt media immediately put this story in print. Roosevelt was so mendacious that he crafted three separate but equally effective factions within the affair-the military, pro-Mossadegh protests, and the angry mob. He had the military force ready to seek out Mossadegh, while also having a mob form violent street demonstrations against Mossadegh. He had agents form opinions that favored communism while, on the other hand, Roosevelt used agents to portray a violent pro-Mossadegh group. Windows were being smashed, as the innocent were beaten by men who either pretended to favor Mossadegh or who followed the actors."

"Roosevelt's mob, the one in favor of overthrowing Mossadegh, became the patriots of Iran. Roosevelt handed one instrumental group $50,000 on the spot. Mossadegh finally ordered his police force to intervene, which increased civil unrest. Crowds, including soldiers, began to shout death to Mossadegh. Eight government buildings would be burnt. A crowd again would head to Mossadegh's house, which was already under military watch. An announcement was made on Radio Tehran that there was now a new prime minister and regime in Iran."

"Mossadegh escaped from his house moments before soldiers broke in. The overthrow was a success! Roosevelt was overwhelmed with joy. Kermit's agents were to be further rewarded. Two would become new cabinet members. It was a chaotic turn of events, but obviously a new government wouldn't disclose information of what truly occurred. Mossadegh would turn himself in. Thus remaining in prison for ten weeks. After release, he was not allowed to leave his village for the duration of his life."

"The CIA gave the new Iranian government five million dollars. The Anglo-Iranian Oil Company would become British Petroleum. They would hold 40% of shares. Five combined American companies would also hold 40%, while the rest went to the Dutch and French Petroleum companies. To keep the smokescreen of nationalization for Iranian oil, the foreigners agreed to share profits fifty-fifty with Iran. The books were still to not be audited, nor not one Iranian was on the board of directors. The CIA successfully disrupted and eliminated Iranian democracy."

"Had no idea huh Jim?"

"Wow!" Jim could not say any other word for a few seconds, "I've been living in a weird place. So far away from the world others see. I am happy you have shown me the other side."

"Some things we have done are very ugly, but we cannot hide it. ... Frederick Douglas said, 'There is not a nation on earth guilty of practices more shocking and bloody than are the people of the United States'. " Dave paused.

"The lawful legitimacy of evil conduct is the essence of what has destroyed the most powerful civilizations. Immoral men thought they were broadening their homeland, where in fact they were slowly destroying it. A distorted truth eliminates the highest intelligence, which eliminates growth and progress."

"Wow. Thank you Dave, I'm a changed man. I'm speechless."

"Spread the word Jim," Dave stood up slowly, "so every Thursday huh."

Jim smiled at Dave and looked at his watch, which read nine o' clock. He then got up in a drunk manner a minute after Dave left and headed back to Sunny Side.

The Engagement

Jim drove home that night, weeping the entire ride home in his Ranger. He vowed to fix everything before he fell asleep. When he woke up with a severe hangover, the humanic persona was lost. He started out Friday morning just as any other, driving his golf cart all around the grounds analyzing beds, flora, and turf. He bumped into Willy five minutes into the cruise.

"What do you say Jimmy?"

"Not much you."

"I gotta tell you, that punk made us 2.2 million cash just by doing that damn date at the convention center."

"I don't know what we're going to do with all that money," said Jim.

At that instant, in the corner of Jim's vision he saw the very pregnant Whitney push mowing her half-acre lawn in the distance. She was mowing all because Tom was so overwhelmed with getting the house ready for the baby.

Something clicked.

Nothing made sense to him. How could Willy not share a dollar with his daughter that her boyfriend had helped him earn? Or at least offer her a position to repay her for Tom's labor.

"Nothing appears as it truly is, Willy," Jim said before he drove off to continue his rounds.

Saturday morning Jim showed up in front of the shack, exactly when Tom was leaving for work. He knew the second Tom left the shack every workday, even when he was working overtime on the weekend. Jim saw the interior light on at five a.m.

Jim walked right up to Tom as he was walking out the door.

Tom spoke first while Jim fumbled a greeting. "Whit's sleeping."

"That's not what I came for. I'm here to talk with you."

"Oh yeah. One of my shrubs is planted to far over on Willy's land. I'm heading out right now. I can't be late." Jim stood silent without making way for Tom to pass.

"I'm not as bad as you think Tom. Is that what you think? I'm here to make your life a living hell. It's not about that. I want to help you. I feel awful for the way I've treated you."

"You just want to apologize to me?"

"Yeah, exactly," Jim smiled.

"About what, I don't understand. It's not like you tried to hurt me or anything. I've made some mistakes and you gave me a hard time for them. I get what I deserve. You don't bother me at all."

"Tom you have to understand, I was wrong in all this."

"I got a second left, I can't be late." Tom looked down at his watch, then looked at Jim with wide eyes, slightly shaking his head up and down.

"Well Tom I'm sorry."

"It's no big deal, but I accept. You had made me feel quite uncomfortable. I don't want to be here, I'm only here because of Whitney."

"Yeah, you haven't deserved what I've put you through."

"It hasn't been fun living around you people. I don't even enjoy walking around the property. There's been a lot of fun had at my expense."

"You've turned into a very good man Tom. I've made mistakes too. I just have always followed what Willy wants."

"I don't think that man will have a change of heart," Tom confidently said.

"That's the real reason I'm talking with you... He's had the mob watching you. He had the Guatemalan's put a curse on you. He's been watching and listening to you on his computer every day. He had a security firm rig up surveillance around the shack."

"What!" Tom appeared struck by an invisible arrow. His neck disappeared within his shoulders.

"See all those extra eyes on those telephone poles," Jim pointed at the microphone and camera that surrounded Tom's house, "They're all pointed at you. Willy can watch you from his very own computer whenever he wants."

"Whitney know about all this?" Tom asked.

"Not a thing."

"I guess that paranoia of someone watching me was really happening. Even a curse? Ha, people only curse themselves."

"The black magic is one thing, but Tom you have to go talk to the police. Willy clearly broke the law. He did not have your consent. I talked to a civil liberties attorney last night and he set me straight."

"We'll see. I appreciate this Jim, apology accepted. Just improve yourself everyday."

Tom left for work. He was so angry. He felt so violated. Tom went over to his sponsor Kevin at the instant he arrived at the shop. He told him the entire true scenario behind the garage. Since sobriety had been reached Tom had not reached a point of anger so severe as this moment. Kevin helped. The sponsor saw Tom was still mad subsequent to the drive in. Kevin chilled him out behind the garage. Tom let it out.

"Anyone to think they could spy on someone and invade their home to find out what the person truly is...

is the shadiest most despicable act. He's got something real messed up inside. What gives him the right!"

Kevin responded, "You know if you report this, things are going to change."

"I know, but I want things to change."

"When are you going to do it Tom?"

"Tomorrow. I have to get a ring after work today, can I leave a little early?"

"Sure. A ring? You sure know how to stir things up."

"My world don't revolve around Willy's." Tom had a large smile across his face.

"Make sure you're doing it for the right reasons."

Tom did not consider a very important thing when constructing his plan, Kissimmee practically revolved around Willy. The main attraction was the Sunny Side Condo's. Tom had no idea Willy grew up with the majority of officers on the police department or the parents of the younger officers.

Anger was released during work. He slammed his shovel into the ground much harder than normal. No grudge was held into the afternoon though. His attention was turned toward the manner in which he was going to propose to Whitney. Thoughts of the one knee position in the house would be more than enough to change the mind. Whitney had wanted to get married forever. Now through the chain of events Tom too knew it was time. There was no doubt Whitney would stand by him through everything. The only uncertainty was Willy's reaction to the engagement or how he would react to having charges filed against him.

Tom was more than confident that if Willy kicked him out, Whitney, the baby, and himself would be better off. The house wasn't a big deal, he would tell Willy he could keep it with all the money and time he put into it. It was just material. The property meant more to Willy. Tom knew Willy would always try his hardest to screw him over and take advantage of the young man for a square foot.

Tom went to the jewelers as soon as he got out an hour early, but he didn't want to spend a lot. Something humble, yet bright like Whitney. The instant he walked in he saw the ring. It was a smaller diamond, yet the shiniest one. He discovered it was four thousand dollars, which he was fine with. They had over ten thousand in savings remaining, but this was something he would only be purchasing once. The money he made from the house in Hartford would make this purchase seem of no consequence. He wrote a check, grabbed the ring, and headed straight home. Anxiety filled his mind, as he could not stop thinking of Whitney's reaction.

It was a slow walk after he parked the truck outside the shack. The sight of Tom's demeanor, which Whitney glanced at from the window, actually brought her concern. She had déjà vu of his drinking days. He seemed troubled. He walked right in. Whitney was sitting at the kitchen table with a puzzled look. He then walked over to her side.

"Whitney we have been through so much. I can't believe what we have become."

"I know. Tom I'm so proud of you. I knew you would become a great man."

"I can't believe you stuck by me through everything. We will get through everything." Shaking ensued. Tom's trembling hand reached in his pocket as he dropped to a knee.

"Will you marry me?"

"Oh, I didn't see this one coming." Whit fanned herself with her hand. "Of course, I will love you forever. This is amazing."

The two kissed and embraced, it went better than Tom could have imagined. It felt right for Tom. If Whitney went into labor, which was any day now, she would now be engaged. Earlier at work, Tom concocted in his head that he could possibly find a justice of the peace before she gave birth. Whitney, however, did not want to do it that way. They discussed when, how, who, and where after the confirmation embrace. "When the baby is born we'll set the date," Whitney said.

Whitney then ran over to her parents' house. Willy was there with Danielle. Whitney came in crying. Willy was ready to make the call, but her tears weren't for what he expected. Whitney's mom was so happy for her, while Willy put on a happy act. Danielle Stanton had no idea of the things Willy had planned for Tom.

The following day was Tom's day to report Willy. Even with the happiness the engagement brought Whitney, he had to stop Willy's comportment. He didn't care if the result tore the father-daughter relationship apart. He wanted to. Tom felt there was nothing that gave Willy the right to invade someone's life, no matter what Tom immaturely did. Tom left Saturday morning on his day off to the police department. He told Whitney he had to square something up.

He walked stiff into the police department. An officer behind glass offered greetings.

"I need to talk to someone about civil liberties."

The officer at the front desk gave Tom a funny look.

"Uh, we have a field sergeant around."

"Yeah anyone that can help," Tom said.

After a minute the sergeant walked up to the waiting area. "Hi there, I'm Sergeant Rogers."

"My name is Thomas Adams."

"What's going on Tom?"

"Can we talk privately?"

"Sure."

"We have room four open."

They walked into interrogation room four. Tom would then devote twenty minutes telling Sergeant Rogers everything. Tom didn't hide anything. He went on all about his disease of alcoholism and its effect on Whitney. He described everything that Uncle Jim disclosed about CSA. All this took Rogers off guard. His wife's family stayed at Sunny Side every year when they flew down from Maine. He stood up, and proceeded to call for his supervisor, Lieutenant Marshall. Before he walked out the door, Rogers told Tom, "We'll get this squared away."

Lieutenant Marshall, of course, knew both Willy and Jim. Indeed, he was a childhood friend and lived behind the condos. As soon as Marshall got off the phone with Rogers he immediately called Willy. Willy was shocked, "You don't write any of this down Marsh. Do you follow? Here's what we're gonna do to that fuck..."

"No problem Willy. I'll let Rogers know, I got you covered."

Within five minutes Rogers came back into room number four with a younger officer. Rogers looked at Tom and told him "We'll get this all squared away, let's take a quick ride in the cruiser, I have something you might like to see."

They escorted Tom out with no hindrance. He was then asked to sit into the back of the squad car.

"Are you arresting me?"

Rogers slammed the door on Tom. He opened the driver's door and sat down.

"Now you're going to see who runs the show out here, punk."

Willy now knew who told Tom. Only Jim knew the magnitude of the surveillance. The phone call Willy received from Lieutenant Marshall, following Tom's interview, disclosed all that Tom had told.

Tom sat silently for five minutes while the cruiser drove to the middle of a doughnut shop parking lot.

Suddenly, a huge light brown Cadillac raced in and skidded alongside the cruiser. The two officers didn't say anything. They simultaneously opened their doors and got out, as the Cadillac breaks screeched. Rogers opened Tom's door, while, at the same time, Willy got out of the passenger side door of the Cadillac, along with two henchmen. Big Willy firmly grabbed Tom by the collar.

"Get the fuck in here!"

Willy was now in the back of the Cadillac sitting next to Tom, with the two mobsters in front. He gave a wave to the officers as they pulled off.

"What the fuck are you thinking Tom. Do you know who you fucked with! First you take my daughter away and then my property. Now you're trying to get me locked up so you can have everything I have bled for."

"I've never wanted anything of yours," Tom quietly spoke, "But your daughter's hand. I have fulfilled your greatest dreams by bringing in all these people to live in your new condos. The ones you built, not your father. I've made you at least a million by volunteering my labor for you and you NEVER EVEN SAID THANK YOU!"

"I DON'T OWE YOU SHIT! YOU SHOULD BE HONORED TO LIVE ON MY LAND."

"I've cleaned myself up, made you a lot of money, put my life savings into your property, am providing a healthy home for your first grandchild, and you treat me like fucking scum! You need to watch me all day. Ha, you want to know everything about me so bad. Do you even know yourself Mr. Stanton?"

"You'll always be a dope head to me. Hector pass me that shit."

Hector handed Willy a metal pipe.

"Hit this shit Tom!"

The pipe was shoved an inch from his mouth.

"Please no, I'm done with that Willy."

"HIT THAT SHIT OR I WILL KILL YOU!"

One quick rip was sparked by Tom. His eyes then closed completely.

Tom didn't return home Saturday night. Whitney had thousands of ill thoughts running through her mind that night, but she managed to eventually fall asleep. She called her mom the minute she woke up alone Sunday morning. "Mom I don't know where Tom is, but...but I think my water just broke!"

"Oh dear! I don't know where you're father or Uncle Jim is either. They've been gone since yesterday.

Dad said he had some emergency business to take care of."

"Really, something happened to Tom, I can feel it. Where ever Dad is, Tom is. I know this! Mom where is Dad."

"What Happened To Tom!"

i Chemtrails Exposed, Peter A. Kirby
ii The Fluoride Deception, Christopher Bryson, Seven Stories Press, 2004
iii A Century of War: Anglo-American Oil Politics and The New World Order, William Engdahl, Pluto Press, 2004, 257
iv The Big Bamboozle, Philip Marshall
v Extreme Prejudice, Susan Lindauer, 2010 pg.61
vi Lindauer, 62
vii Lindauer, 163
viii Lindauer, 66
ix A Power Governments Cannot Suppress, Howard Zinn, pg. 195
x A Power Governments Cannot Suppress, Howard Zinn, pg. 164

[xi] A Power Governments Cannot Suppress, Howard Zinn, pg. 75
[xii] A Power Governments Cannot Suppress, Howard Zinn, pg. 115